D0492666

EARTHING THE WORD

Earthing the Word

Selected writings from *The Furrow*
by
Thomas G. Waldron

the columba press

First published in 2014 by
the columba press
55A Spruce Avenue,
Stillorgan Industrial Park,
Blackrock, Co. Dublin

Cover by David Mc Namara, C.Ss.R.
Origination by The Columba Press
In association with *The Furrow*,
in which all of the articles originally appeared.

Printed by Scandbook, Sweden

ISBN 978 1 78218 147 7

Acknowledgements
The scripture quotations contained herein are from the New
Revised Standard Version Bible, copyright © 1989, Division of
Christian Education of the National Council of Churches of Christ
in the USA. Used by permission. All rights reserved.

Contents

INTRODUCTION

Per Cortesia

In his shimmering essay, *Real Presences*, George Steiner rejects aggressive deconstruction of classical texts in favour of their courteous reception. *Per cortesia* is the first manner of the reader-interpreter in seeking to understand and enjoy any artistic work. The critique and further analysis may follow but they should serve to enable the reader/viewer/listener to understand, evaluate and, more deeply, to be critically as well as courteously receptive to a genuinely artistic work.

In a competitive and combative world where high-powered marketing, with its own brand of creativity, can make it so difficult to distinguish trash from treasure, and where critics – with a responsibility to discriminate, and so to educate – are too easily tempted by what might be termed analytic reduction, the call to courteous, critical attention not only for recognised works of art but for interesting and promising newcomers has the ring of sanity. An outstanding quality of Tommy Waldron's approach to life was his courteous attention to and reception of literary and other artistic classics, particularly the Hebrew and Christian scriptures. All this nourished his courteous attention to and reception of people, his courteous attention to and reception of God.

People before causes

In meeting, reading and listening to Tommy Waldron one never detected a trace of the ideologue. His commitments to faith and Church, to truth and beauty, to justice and peace were never distorted into uncritical causes or angry campaigning. People in all their weaknesses and ambiguities, as well as in their potential and real goodness came first, not causes. This could be interpreted as weakness in the polarised situations of the Irish Church and Irish society during his influential years as pastor, preacher and writer. Yet to listen to him or read him in the ranting years of the seventies, eighties and nineties was to recognise a voice of sanity and of strength. In the midst of the divisive debates on law and morality, through the turbulence of the Northern Troubles, during clerical sex scandals, Tommy Waldron concentrated on the people in his constituency who were affected and left the headline elements to others.

Not that he thought all the headlines irrelevant, still less untrue, but his sense of people and his gifts of caring for the immediately afflicted and affected determined his priorities. In parish, pulpit and confessional, at baptisms, weddings and funerals, in his regular meditative essays for radio, in his retreats and in his prestigious sermons at the Knock Annual Vigil, his attention to real people, with ordinary or extraordinary concerns, in word and image, in story, in inflection of voice and in bodily posture and gesture, shone through.

The encoded but still vital remains of this devotion to people of all ages and backgrounds constitute the primary value of this selection of his writings, drawn from *The Furrow*. As a trustee of that journal and a trusted friend and confidant of both its editors, J. G. McGarry and Ronan Drury, he influenced and was influenced by the most effective Irish Catholic publication of the last fifty years.

Flesh made word
The baby's first words, the child's first sentences, the developing, sometimes riotous vocabulary of the adolescent were all a delight to Tommy Waldron who so loved the words not as dictionary components but as struggling bodily attempts to communicate between body-spirits. The very fleshiness of words was to be savoured like good wine, perhaps sometimes for their own sake, but principally in the delicate and fragile reaching out to the other body-spirit. His care for words was a carefully honed skill of mind and mouth. From his school days to his death days, so cruelly focused on his gradual loss of speech, he exemplified St James's model not just in truth-telling but in the beautiful healing way of telling.

All this caring communication had a history in his own family of course, but more formally in his educational interests in languages and literature. He was one of the outstanding scholars of his era in his BA and MA studies in English Language and Literature, had a fluent knowledge of the Irish language and went on to study French to the point of becoming a teacher in that subject at second level. His wide reading of novels, drama and poetry extended his mind and sensibility as a teacher and pastor. His precise and yet imaginative choice of word and simile, his use of story and parable, his arresting connections between biblical and domestic events, as in his reflections on the Mayo woman and the Jewish man, his deployment of the Ugly Duckling fable in a baptismal homily, were all born of a heart, imagination, mind and vocabulary schooled by Shakespeare, Eliot and Heaney as well as by pupils and neighbours, parishioners and penitents in the narrow triangle of his priestly work between Headford, Tuam and Claremorris.

Performance artist

Readings by major and minor poets are a phenomenon of our time and by and large an enjoyable one. Most good poetry needs to be read aloud at least occasionally and if possible by the poet, who may not always equal technically and aesthetically a Richard Burton, but puts his personal and vocal mark on the poem's music and meaning. The 'performance poets', as they are sometimes called, belong to a wider range of performance or performing artists, notably of course actors. To this broad category priests as teachers, preachers and celebrants of the liturgy might be loosely assigned, with the liturgical religious ritual background to the development of theatre also to be borne in mind. In Tommy Waldron's case the assignment would be far from loose. In celebrating baptism and Eucharist as at weddings and funerals, he was so often producer/director as well as best supporting actor to Christ and the Spirit, to the marrying and the grieving. The script, partly the Church's and partly his own scribbles, was performed with all the skill of his own talent and schooling and all the conviction of his own faith, hope and love. Some of his best work even in this restricted selection needs to be heard aloud, particularly in the voice we no longer enjoy.

Writing and speaking into God

Writing is a critical part of the human Christian search, the search for meaning and truth, the search for community and love. So is speaking. They belong together, at least for somebody of Tommy Waldron's generation, education and personal gifts. For him they were also human and divine graces of faith and hope and love. To write and to speak were acts of trust in the words and their meaning, in the readers and audience, in the ultimate significance of words and persons resting in the Ultimate Word and Persons of God. The process of writing and speaking led him to that ultimate destiny; it became a writing and speaking into God. The self-surrender in search of the precise and sensitive words to discover and communicate the truth to the audience addressed was a saving act for him and for them. Redeeming the time, in one of his favourite Eliot allusions, involved as for all wordsmiths redeeming and saving the language and so participating in redeeming self and audience, entering into the creative and redeeming work of God.

For the writer and speaker who was Tommy Waldron, the Spirit of God was embracing the performer and the performance all the more in his allowing the scriptural texts to nourish and inhabit him in study and prayer. It is the context of all Christian writing and speaking, if only occasionally managed by most. It is a costly embrace, as Tommy knew well. Despite his general cheerful demeanour he knew suffering well, that of others as well as his own, and could speak of it authentically and consolingly. One of his favourite books in recent years was *Etty*, a remarkable diary by a Holocaust victim. His reading and rereading of that book, as reflected in his speaking and writing, undoubtedly led him to reading and writing into God, to prayer. Indeed he prayed regularly to her, as certainly now in the company of the saints.

Perhaps it was this companionship with the suffering in life and in death that enabled him to bear so admirably his own painful and lingering death. In earlier times he would quote a phrase of Henri de Lubac to the effect that we all suffer badly. He may well have known a deeper truth of this as he was fatally attacked in his most delicate gift of speech by ravaging mouth cancer, but he did not impose the horror of it on his friends.

May this collection of his writings remind his many friends and admirers how a gifted, sane and saintly man gave voice, in their darkness and his, to the true light. Through them, these friends of so many generations, and one hopes many new readers, may his work continue to influence a wider public and help to dissipate some of the continuing darkness.

Enda McDonagh

The Sign of the Scallop Shell

Vol. 30, No. 10, October 1979

Dante said that pilgrims, properly speaking, were those who went to the shrine of St James at Compostela. Of the others, those who went to Jerusalem and brought back bits of palm were Palmers, those who went to Rome were Romeos, but those who carried the scallop shell of St James and went to and from Compostela were pilgrims. And so the scallop shell became the badge of the pilgrim, though with the irony of a long history, *Coquilles St Jacques* appeared on menus far removed from the beaten path of pilgrimage.

The pilgrim carried his shell and the houses where he could stay were also marked by a shell. This month Pope John Paul II comes to Ireland as a pilgrim and we are fixing the scallop shell above the door.

It is right that the same emblem should mark those who travel and those who meet the traveller, for the pilgrim and host are essential to the pilgrimage. They affect and change each other, enriching each other with difference, strengthening their sameness. The pilgrimage and the hospitality, the movement and the resting place are both founded on the same faith. That faith grows stronger at their meeting, and in the new strength they give each other they move on closer to the shrine they seek.

Kenosis

Pilgrimage is a sort of death. The pilgrim comes to the crowd and travels with it but at the end he moves out of the crowd to aloneness in the presence of God. It is a journey to that moment of being just oneself – the spare self, separated for that moment from all people and things and histories. There is no past, all is present, and it is a moment of judgement and of love. All the accretions of time drop away and we are received and loved as we are, with 'just me' as my own total recommendation. There is no longer any pose or stance possible or needed; no position, no possession matters because they do not exist at this moment of judgement. And we are sure of being received and not rejected – for the place of pilgrimage is a place of promise, the promise that *kenosis* ensures entry, acceptance, communion and new life.

For Pope John Paul the terminus of his pilgrimage is when he kneels at the shrine alone. His moment of arrival is not when he is greeted and joins us, but the moment when he leaves the others, us all, and kneels at the gable wall at Knock. At that moment he is no longer Pope. To that moment he journeys.

At that moment he is one of us, not greater or less or more loved, but one of the children committed to Mary. Like any of us he will kneel there and his kneeling will say: 'This is me.' For this is the end of every pilgrimage, the presentation of the essential self to God. Pilgrimage is a movement towards discovery. It is a presentation that is wordless for the great moment is always the moment before words. The final discovery is too great for words, and beyond all telling. For Pope or anyone, this is journey's end – oneself, one's mere self, merely Karol Wojtyla, present to God. But God knows and loves.

Communion

Our journey is graced by his. The Pope's pilgrimage tells us the truth – that our journey is like his. He doesn't come to wash our feet but to offer his pilgrim's feet to be washed with ours, and to echo again the words of his predecessor, 'Lord, not only my feet but also my hands and my head.' These are not the words of Peter, Pope, but of Peter, Christian. Suddenly we discover that John Paul is one of us, and Peter is one of us, and Francis of Assisi, going down to Compostela, is one of us. For at the wall we are Everyman with the words Karol Wojtyla gave to St John as he spoke to Our Lady, 'I am John the Fisherman. There isn't much in me to love.' We are, all of us, 'the living men who inhabit the single room to meet Christ and get new heart'.

Pilgrimage is like a Mass, liturgy of Word and Eucharist. It is faith formulated by feet, every step a profession. The slow walk of the old, the pained movement of the sick are strong statements of a creed. There is offering of time and thanks, of privacy, of energy, offering of bone and mind, offering of power and offering of powerlessness. Your everyday paten bears slighter bread.

The disparate elements from all the disparate places fill the ciborium of pilgrimage and the Mass has an intensity forged by feet and distance. Each pilgrim adds himself and his accumulated meaning to the pilgrimage Mass and John Paul, pilgrim, will add his meaning to the Mass John Paul, Pope, says on 30 September.

The Journey

Pilgrimage is journey. You have to be from somewhere else – Rome or Kiltimagh – to be a pilgrim at Knock. It is rooted in movement and was associated with prayer outside and before Christianity. One could, of course, retire to one's room and pray, and indeed Our Lord pressed upon us the claim of secret prayer. For most of the year the Pope will, as Chesterton imagined him, pray in his private chapel before dawn or battle break. But while a man must not be much in journeyings, there is no doubt that journey and place have always helped people to pray, and have themselves become part of people's prayers. Almost everything recorded of the Holy Family is journey and the only little bit of the recorded boyhood of Christ is pilgrimage. I have no doubt that the walk and talk on the road affected the breaking of bread at Emmaus. And indeed there are medieval carvings of the journey to Emmaus which show Christ wearing the scallop shell.

One might say it is only human that journey and history and association and companionship heighten prayer. But it isn't 'only human' – it is so and has to be so because people are like that. A hundred years of talking together and walking together to Knock, of praying together and alone at Knock – two rosaries of years, they count for something. To walk where so many pilgrims have come in penance, in thanksgiving, in despair, in search of healing – one feels the blessing of their presence still. *Sunt lacrimae rerum* (There are tears for things), and there is grace in such tears. Our own words borrow faith from the echo of older prayers and other feet. And while the grace of God cannot be limited or confined, still heaven and men have agreed that the composition of place adds something to prayer. People have always chosen special places for prayer, God has marked special places with his favour. The pilgrim to Knock or Częstochowa or Guadalupe – adds one more pebble to the heaped-up experience of humanity – that pilgrimage is a way to meet God. Not every bush burns.

The Pilgrim Church

Pilgrimage is, of course, a symbol of the journey to the eschaton. The caravan moves across the desert through heat and wind and danger, from oasis to oasis, to the place of no more journey. Home safe, with now no need of courage, no straining to see another oasis. There is at the end of travelling the joy of final arrival – faith passed away, hope passed away, the kingdom has come and will not pass away.

The Church is a pilgrim church, making its way through time to eternity. Like the single pilgrim it discovers itself on the way, its meaning, its faults, its riches, its resources. Like the single pilgrim on the way, it learns humility and renews itself. And it is always on the way and *semper reformanda* (always to be reformed).

But that is the only way to make a pilgrimage – because you need to and you know you need to. I think it is the pilgrim church Karl Rahner means when he says the Church is exploring its own mystery and discovering its unsuspected depths and realising with a growing love the guidance of God who seeks to conform it to his own death and Resurrection. Conformation. Pilgrimage gets us all into shape.

The Personal Story

The Church, the group, moves along its pilgrim road, and the individual is never submerged, but sustained. There is unity without loss of identity. Chaucer with his most famous group of pilgrims wasn't far from the truth of it. One thinks of *The Canterbury Tales* as a unit, but each one's story is his own – Knight or Wyf or Miller. Every pilgrimage is a collection of stories and each of us goes to Lough Derg or Croagh Patrick or Knock with his own story – the story only he can tell, the story he will tell only to Mary, to God. It is said that Chaucer made his own pilgrimage to Canterbury when his wife Philippa was ill. His prayers to Our Lady run easily across eight hundred years.

Queen of comfort
– but oh when I think of my guilt before him and thee!
Lady bright you know me.
Tell me how I can have your favour and your help.
O fresh flower, mercy lives forever in you.
The world waits ever on your goodness
For you never fail anyone in need.

'The Knight's Tale',
The Canterbury Tales,
Geoffrey Chaucer

Those are some words of Geoffrey Chaucer's story.

Pope John Paul will come with his own story and his own way of telling it. In his pilgrim coming he will try to imitate the self-emptying of Christ 'who became poor'. He will come to her whom the Connaught prayer calls the Queen of the Poor. In the way of that prayer he will ask her to whisper a word for him and to lead him to judgement.

We have our part in his coming to that moment of recognition and discovery and new strength. For, on the pilgrimage we sustain one another and are lifted up and carried on by the companionship of need and faith. So we must not dwell only on the gift his coming brings us. We must remember his dependence, and pray for him, that his pilgrimage and ours may end where pilgrim and host are finally both at home and together.

The time that my journey takes is long and
the way of it is long
the traveller has to knock at every alien door to
come to his own, and one has to wander through all
the outer worlds to reach the innermost shrine at the end.

'The Time That My Journey Takes',
Gitanjali,
Rabindranath Tagore

For Yours is the Kingdom
– *The Beatitudes*
Vol. 33, No. 5, May 1982

It is hard to imagine Christ being satisfied with a draw. He must sometimes settle for it and sometimes accept defeat but he is committed to victory, not partial victory but total victory, not immediate victory but final victory. The religion which we call by his name, it too has a Kerry, a Liverpool, a Welsh quality – a disbelief in ultimate defeat or limited achievement. The kingdom will come.

I do not flippantly use the language of sport to express mysteries. Paul is my distant ancestor and it is remarkable how much the language of people's popular interests – the language of where their hearts and purest commitments are – is the language of salvation. The sports pages reflect metaphorically the final reality of struggle, the cardinal virtues of belief, confidence and support, the possibility of losing, and victory and celebration.

They reflect too mankind's desire for complete victory – the popular *Weltanschauung,* the World Cup, the World Series, the World Championship. This again is the dimmed reflection of Christ's world concern. For God's story begins with the whole world and the all-mankind of Eden; Christ comes as the light which is to enlighten every man, and his disciples are given a mission to all nations. The chalice of suffering will become the cup of victory which we shall finally sup from, when the tens and tens of thousands gather at the Supper of the Lamb.

So often the people – the crowd, that big flock of sheep which Jesus pities, that clutch of ungathered chickens – unconsciously foreshadow destiny and the divine plan. This is not remarkable because the kingdom that is to come is not only God's but theirs. It is the kingdom they long for, dream of, pray for, a kingdom of justice, love and peace, a kingdom beyond the wear and tear of this life.

And it is their kingdom. It is not a kingdom of small groups but for all. The invitation and mission of Christ is to everybody. Christianity's small groups were never just for group therapy or for the sake of the group, but for the benefit of all. Carmelite nun or Trappist monk are mine and all for me. The Church has always with sure instinct suspected groups which denied salvation to the common people. The light is for Everyman. Christ died for the people who read the sports pages, the people of the eighth station, the people he fed.

That's one reason why I find it hard to accept that the Beatitudes were addressed to the disciples only – which is one of the theories about them. Christ was concerned with the mass market. Even if he went after the one sheep he was still shepherd of a hundred – and had other sheep too. And Pope John Paul, wondering about his visit to the people of Brazil, reached for the Beatitudes: 'When I thought of the way in which I should present myself to the inhabitants of Brazil, I felt the duty of presenting above all the teachings of the eight Beatitudes.' Like master, like man.

Of course the Pope is talking about content, but the very cut of the Beatitudes is for the people, the ready-to-wear market. They have the ring of the proverb about them and mankind dearly loves its proverbs. We seem to like our wisdom in metre and in short – the iambic is the beat of the heart. The truths we do grasp we like to be enshrined and accessible.

So I prefer the theory that Christ, like the Jewish rabbis of his time – and like good teachers of all times – summarised his teaching and put it in a way that wooed and gratified the ear and the memory. The Beatitudes were a sort of mental phylactery designed to wear well.

The rabbis liked to provide catechisms, and that was where I first met the Beatitudes – in a little book popular in National School, *Catechism Notes*. There were the eight of them, and the Seven Dolours, and the Twelve Fruits of the Holy Spirit. They were for grown men of ten and eleven, and we learned them as the man who composed them meant them to be learned – by repetition and by heart. They were made for that – all beginning with the word 'blessed', all in two parts, the first and last in the present tense and promising the Kingdom of Heaven, the intermediate six in the future – two 'ises' and six 'shalls'. It is nice to think that after two thousand years the same tool of learning had not lost its edge. It's the old pleasure and strength of the formula. It's in the writings of Homer and of Virgil, in *Beowulf* and the *Fiannaíocht*. Humanity has always used it for its epics and the Beatitudes are the story of man's journey to God – of man's lost obedience and the fruit of that forbidding tree, the Cross.

Later I came to preach the Beatitudes, making a sermon of the Sermon, fleshing them out as they flesh out the two great commandments. The Beatitudes need this, for each of them is like a closed concertina, fold and fold compressed but ready to open into long rich meaning. Yet one was conscious as one did it of the pejorative phrase, 'preacher's use of scripture'. That used to be said by scholars who dealt faithfully with the written bones and who mildly despised fanciful flesh on the skeletal frame. It was a time when the flesh was despised.

But then T. S. Eliot especially made it respectable to say that there was more in poetry than its writer knew, that it bore meanings that awaited discovery. And biblical scholarship began to say that there was an oral gospel before there was a written one and that the scripture was anyway simply a summary of what Christ had preached. So the scholar had his place and restored original grace to the preacher, and the preacher realised that he did not need the support of marching footnotes to justify every meaning that the Word of God yielded to meditation or imagination.

The Beatitudes are the essential good news but I remember them as frightening. I read them first as threat, not promise. For me they were conditional sentences, 'If you are not pure in heart you shall not see God.' Religion is not obviously good news, especially not to the young. A little girl who told me she spoke to God often (she used to say 'Shut up, You') may have many who understand her and would say the same – if they dared. The opposite to the good news can be very bad news indeed – pain, punishment, loss, being outcast, being damned. We can seem to be caught in a game which we never asked to play and in which the punishment for losing is so terrible that it vitiates all hope and joy in winning. Religion then becomes a set of precautionary measures and heaven only an escape – the mere absence of hell.

Promises not threats

My change to seeing the Beatitudes as promises, not threats, was a function not so much of Vatican II but of aging. Aging often confers both wisdom and grace. Youth is a time of hope and promise in most areas but in the spiritual area it is often a time of threat. Perhaps it has (or had – I may be simply reflecting an era) to do with a time when one is so clearly under authority and when the person is under attack from a confusion of feelings. The voice of the merciful Christ, of the wise and comprehending and compassionate Lord, is not the *cantus firmus* (fixed song) of adolescence. For youth the serious God is restraining and sometimes minatory. There is at least the suspicion of a thunderbolt up his sleeve.

Strangely, a little later, when the rosy turns to speckled and mottled, the theology of fear yields to a theology of hope and possibility. As you realise in yourself the need for salvation and what that salvation must mean in personal terms, at that moment you realise that this is what Christ is promising. How could God have come upon the earth to increase our fears, to underline impossibility or to preach an elitist salvation? Anxiety and hopelessness and exclusivity we manufacture at home, we need no visiting God for these. Christ could not have come, seen, helped, and loved people and then bowed out of their lives saying, 'Ah, God help them.'

There is only one news that is good, and that is the word that all the good that is in us, as dream or desire or possibility, will yet come into being. We are trapped, oppressed, powerless, but aware and offering, and we need to be. The good which is in us, which we can do, which we can be – this must not die; it demands life. We are not destined to be unfinished stories. We need a saviour. We need a kingdom. We cry for completion.

The Beatitudes are God's answer to the cry he implanted in us, God's catalogue of possible completions. Salvation is available, and is happening at this moment and to us. The Beatitudes introduce a note of sober, exultant and sustaining reality into what was once dream or nightmare. They are promise but current reality too – the pilgrim church has part of its journey over, the people of God are already future. Hell is a fading fire for 'a royal race and a princely people'.

And the terms of the Beatitudes are concrete and basic, strong, true and assured – we shall see, we shall possess, we shall have, we shall obtain, be filled, be comforted, be called the children of God, and the kingdom will be ours. There is nothing hazy or visionary or doubtful. We have here the strict promise of God; this is a covenant on the edge of final fulfilment.

And this will happen not for vaguely defined, shadowy wraiths but for people with strong, hard profiles, people we knew, people we can be, people we are – merciful people, gentle people, people whose passion is justice, people whose passion is peace, honest and decent people, people upset by the inequities of their world, poor people, suffering people, weak people. The Beatitudes are the ultimate charter of Everyman. They are the measured statements of God, cost calculated, term set, delivery secured on date due. They are hard statements – they are not metaphors to crumble under pressure. Each is like a rock.

The Beatitudes and the Temptations

It may be by accident or design that Matthew sets the Beatitudes almost immediately after the temptations in his narrative. Nowhere is the difference between the kingdom of this world and the kingdom that is to come so pointed. The Beatitudes read like Christ's direct rebuttal of the gospel according to Satan. Satan offers things and instant rewards. Oddly enough or not, what he offers is remarkably close to what J. K. Galbraith in *The Afflict Society* names as the function of wealth – power and name, dominion: these are Satan's miracles. Christ even in his miracles proclaims a different vision – he brings life from death, sight from blindness, movement from immobility, healing from sickness. The Beatitudes are about people raised to new life; the temptations are about how to succeed in business.

Satan must have been a puzzled angel as he left Christ. His suspicions were confirmed as to who Christ was but he was even less sure what that means. C. S. Lewis once said that a lower order of being cannot conceive how a higher order of being sees, judges, acts – because the higher inhabits a country, breathes an air, has a vision, lives a life of which the lower being has no experience. Satan's offers to Christ are instinct with Satan's misconceptions of what God or goodness is like. Christ's values are without meaning for Satan. Satan can see for the human being no hunger that is not of the belly kind, no power that is not physical, no possessions that are not tangible. For Satan man is a creature of the present, for Christ we are people of the future.

So Satan's promise is instant in its satisfaction. But it bears the marks of its paternity – it is for personal aggrandisement, it is given on condition that you sell yourself and, like many of our special offers, it is 'for a limited time only'. The blessedness of the Beatitudes is by contrast total and forever. It is the fulfilment of Boethius's classical definition of happiness. There is no fear of loss. Christ's giving is beyond the power of time or temporalities. His giving is the new and everlasting covenant. In Hosea, God had said: 'I will take back my corn and my wine … I will retrieve my wool, my flax.' But now with Christ there is no taking back. The gifts of the Beatitudes are complete and absolute. It is the fulfilment of the promise made later in Hosea:

> I will take you for my wife forever … in righteousness and in justice,
> in steadfast love, and in mercy … in faithfulness; and you shall
> know the Lord …
> I will sow him for myself in the land.
> And I will have pity on Lo-ruhamah [Not pitied],
> and I will say to Lo-ammi [Not my people], 'You are my people';
> and he shall say, 'You are my God.'
>
> Hos 2:19–23

The final gift is being, or having citizenship, in the kingdom of heaven. Satan's gifts are commerce and they are accretions – bits added on to the person. Christ's are covenant and they are integral.

Even specifically the Beatitudes reject the world system of the temptations. The hunger which deeply matters is the hunger for righteousness – and part of that is the hunger to see that the hungry are fed not as a bribe but as a matter of right. The earth will indeed be given, but to the gentle – they who watched the rats race will receive what the rats raced for, because they will respect and will do no violence to the earth. A kingdom will be received but it is the kingdom of heaven and its recipients will be the poor and the suffering. The power of God will be used – not for catching the mountebank but for the comforting of those saddened by the evil of the world, and for the reward of those who tried to make peace. And heaven is won, not bought; it is a matter of being, not having. Christ in the Beatitudes rejects the instant acquisition that Satan offered. In the divine economy, in God's usual way, there is no totally unearned income. In Bonhoeffer's phrase, there is no such thing as cheap grace. Discipleship is costly. Heaven is not as easy as falling off a log – or jumping off a pinnacle. Heaven is goodness slow-ripening into sanctity. Heaven is long suffering crowned with peace. Heaven is earnest prayer become lasting achievement. Heaven is hunger finally satisfied at the Supper of the Lamb. Heaven is the home of which all other homes were pale images – the place that our hearts have spent a lifetime beating for, hoping for, believing in:

> My people will abide in a peaceful habitation,
> in secure dwellings, and in quiet resting places.
>
> Isa 32:18

The Blessed in Heaven

The Beatitudes are really the demography of heaven, its population by categories, a census of the saints. Who are the Blessed? These are the Blessed. They inhabit the many mansions that make up his Father's house, but they are all at home. These are Christ's own who in one way or another have confessed him before men, who bear one mark or another of the Crucified – his poverty, his pain, his mercy, his hunger, his gentleness, his peace, his generosity. These are God's people at journey's end.

But they're not weary pilgrims. These are the victorious at home. Imagine them in a room together. The assurance and approbation of victory invests each of them. They are confirmed in joy. As in every victory, there is speech of delight and praise. Here there is nothing abrasive. There is only delicious unity and gratitude. They are more perfectly what they were in life – now all for others, with no trace whatever of selfishness or competition or jealousy.

It is a gathering of total generosity. To their delight they all find here in each other the people they championed on earth. The final comfort of the mourners is to find here the poor for whom they mourned. Those who thirsted for justice are ecstatic to meet here, and happy the gentle and downtrodden whose liberation they hungered for. The persecuted will at last meet the merciful. Heaven is like that, if we can believe the Beatitudes – not just us with our goodness but those our goodness was for. We save each other.

In that room there could be surprise too. The people of the Beatitudes as Christ portrays them are quite different in character. When they meet they will find present some who, they thought, were opposed to them on earth. Quite obviously those who hunger and thirst after justice often have little patience with the peace-makers or the meek or the merciful. Here on earth, too, there are people with the same hunger and the same vision who travel by different roads and directions, and who mistake one another for enemies. They take opposite ways of reaching the same goal, or they travel the same road walled off from one another by colour or creed or nationality or ideology. People who were passionate in their differences and perhaps saw themselves as irreconcilable will find that their God is well pleased with both his children and they will share the same reward. They will be delighted to find they are brothers and regret only – if there can be regret in heaven – that they did not come to know each other sooner. God will reward their honesty and their passion as it dawns fully on them in his light that their real achievement is not on earth but in heaven.

'Theirs is the kingdom of heaven' – the promise of the first Beatitude and the last. It is not, I think, accidental that the Beatitudes open and close with the promise of the kingdom. The kingdom is the all-embracing concept. Indeed, Christ's last public statement of his mission is 'I am a king but mine is not a kingdom of this world.' In that kingdom are his gathered people, the 'immortal wheat' of Traherne harvested. In the Beatitudes they reflect each other's goodness, in the kingdom they reflect and mirror each other's glory. The first and last Beatitudes suggest the enveloping grace of the kingdom where light is added to light, to light, to light – the 'immortal diamond' of Hopkins ('That Nature is a Heraclitean Fire and of the Comfort of the Resurrection', G. M. Hopkins) in its final setting, the many-faceted Christ.

Christ, First of the Blessed

For Christ is there too, the pleased teacher of the sermon with successful pupils – but much more than that. Here is the vine and its branches, here is the Mystical Body and its members, here Christ is with his friends. They are each the embodiment of part of his goodness and he is the embodiment of all their goodness. For Christ is not just the teacher of the Beatitudes but their exemplar and first model.

On the Cross Christ exemplifies the first part of each Beatitude. He is the poor – who was without power and had nowhere to lay his head. He is the gentle who broke no bruised reed. He has mourned over Jerusalem and longed to gather his people to him. He hangs between heaven and earth because he has hungered and thirsted for what is right. He is merciful even as he dies. He is the pure in heart who set his face towards Jerusalem and accepted the chalice of his Father's will. He came with the promise of peace and peace was his greeting. He is the persecuted one, the Suffering Servant, 'for our faults struck down in death' (Isa 53:8). Suddenly the good thief recognised him and knew that his was the kingdom.

Christ rose to inherit that kingdom. All the Beatitudes find their most complete fulfilment in the Risen Christ. If no other proof were present of the reality of Christ's Resurrection and divinity, the difference between the one like us who was in agony and the one who now appears calm in the power and certain identity of God might well suffice. Christ risen is divinely assured but now separate from the human condition, 'his soul's anguish over'. He is one with the Father and fully the Son of God in his own being. He has entered into possession of the kingdom prepared for him. The earth is his and the times and the ages.

Our fulfilment, since we have been baptised into his death, will be like Christ's. The prophecy 'ye shall be like gods' – the destiny of man in Eden – culminates in the Blessed. Christ is all those blessed people, and summation of the Beatitudes. We, of course, are partial people pursuing our limited and limiting vocations. We have the aspirations to do everything but the realisation that we are circumscribed by time and energy and ability and a host of other limitations. Sometimes too, despite the aspiration, we sin; we go, as God said, into 'exile for want of perception'. Most of us are smallholders tilling a patch of ground.

But the aspiration is our window looking out onto the immense possibility that baptism and Eucharist and Passion and Resurrection prepare us for. We plod to point Omega but we are more conscious of the plodding than Christ is. For him we are the Blessed he spoke of, following where he has led.

The Christian is future-governed. Christ the exemplar of the Beatitudes is the exemplar of our destiny. For each of us who lives in some way the first part of some Beatitude he is, in Rilke's words, 'the coming one, imminent from all eternity, the future one, the final fruit of a tree whose leaves we are' (*Letters to a Young Poet*, R.M. Rilke).

We are easily aware and persuaded of this in the case of the saints – those we read about, those we knew. They are obviously Beatitude people marked by the signs of faith. These are the people Austin Farrer writes of: 'Men whose words are like their faces, and their faces like their hearts and their hearts printed with the Cross of Christ.'

These are the champions. But the Beatitudes are about the many, the ordinary. They're about the people you'd like to see in heaven, I'd like to see in heaven. And if we can see the goodness which we should love to preserve, perfect, and enjoy forever, I think Christ will be no less aware than we.

I want to see there the young plumber who refused the extra wage I offered and asked me to give it to Trócaire. Blessed are the merciful …

I want to see the girl who refused the £10,000 a year job in favour of her friend who had seen the advertisement first. Blessed are the clean of heart …

I want to see the old alcoholic priest of whom a man said to me, 'He's so good that when I get to heaven I'll have a crick in my neck looking up at him.' Blessed are the gentle …

And I do not think that Christ exhausted the Beatitudes when he named only eight. So I want to see Tom for his sense of humour, Dick for his kindness, Harry for his patience.

There are all sorts and conditions of people who must be there. There will be Christians and non-Christians. The Christians perhaps offer their goodness more consciously, for they are privileged, in Joan Didion's phrase, to be 'the elected representatives of the invisible city'. The non-Christians are those Christ was equally aware of, those not of this fold. All the goodness there is, all the pain there is – small decencies, small mercies, great lives, great sorrows – he takes and marks for salvation. He exalts all our virtues into passports to his kingdom. All people are his people, for Christ came to save the world.

So the denouement of the Beatitudes is the Wedding Feast of the Lamb. It is to this that they point and lead. The throngs who will sit down at the feast are the people nominated by Christ in Galilee. In the Beatitudes Christ displayed so many wedding garments for our wearing. Each guest wears now and forever a garment woven in time. The bride wears the dazzling white linen which 'is made of the good deeds of the saints'. The angel proclaims the final beatitude: 'Happy are those who are invited to the wedding feast of the Lamb.' The Blessed enter their kingdom. It is eschaton (end-time) and pleroma (fullness), the fullness of time. The lone voice which in Palestine said, 'Blessed are the …' is answered by 'the voice of a great multitude, like the sound of many waters and like the sound of mighty thunderpeals, crying out, "Hallelujah! For the Lord our God the Almighty reigns."'

A Venture into Journalling

Vol. 37, No. 5, May 1986

There are fashions even in saints. I think St Joseph got more notice twenty years ago. The feast of St Joseph the Worker came then as a sort of Mayday signal to drown out the Internationale and guns and drums in Red Square. But the Church seems less afraid of Communism now and St Joseph is leading a quiet life, making an annual appearance for the Holy Family photograph.

But we must be underrating him hugely. Oh, he's mentioned – but he's becoming just a name, not a name to conjure with, however, and in his statues he seems so often like Gilbert's young man 'with a poppy or a lily in his medieval hand' (*The Aesthete*, W.S. Gilbert).

Yet the gospel's few overt glimpses of him are glimpses of someone steady, fair, capable, a just man, a man with an instinct for truth and for action, a man who could read signs and make do and who could size up a situation, knowing when to go and when to return, knowing who to trust. Now the gospel doesn't say much about him, but I like to think that we see him many times and hear a lot about him from Christ who knew him well.

Christ must have picked up the idea of 'father' most of all from the man of the house in Nazareth. I think that behind the word 'father' whenever Christ uses it he sees the face of Joseph, the man who picked him up and carried him on his shoulders and showed him the sheep.

It is common with us at a certain age in life to look back with great thanks for our parents and with a new perception of them as people. I don't know the age – it is different for different people I suppose – but perhaps it is really after the death of the parent. We in strange ways enter into a new possession of parents when they die. I remember a girl telling me with amazement that in the few minutes after she witnessed her father's death, she found herself speaking to him and calling him by his Christian name, and finding that she knew him in a new way now and he was 'somebody my own age'. And the experience was one full of love and joy.

There would have been no fewer memories in Christ's private world than in any of our own. There was an old rhyme I remember from *The Annals of Saint Anne* forty years ago:

Bernard of the monasteries
Thomas of the books
Met angels in the hallways
Pale wonder in their looks

Joseph of the tool chest
Have you no pride at all?
'I kissed God's lips at bedtime
When God was very small.'

Not a memorable verse, you might say, and probably inaccurately remembered, but I think now with the germ of a truth I might have too long neglected – Joseph's relationship with Jesus. (And I don't know why I feel so apologetic about the verse. We can get too sophisticated. After all, when Sartre wondered how he would paint Our Lady, if he were a painter, he thought of her looking at her child – the only woman ever, he said, who looked at her baby and saw God.)

So Christ would have remembered Joseph in all the ways anyone who has grown up in a family remembers his father. And very clearly his memories were very good. There is obviously no conflict between his vision of his heavenly Father and his pictures of Joseph. There is the love, the trust, the relationship of 'Father if it be possible', 'Father forgive them', 'Father into your hands.' This is Abba, the one you'd turn to – someone who'd make sure you'd have bread on the table, someone who'd forgive, someone who'd mind you. 'Give us this day our daily bread, deliver us from evil.'

Joseph's face and hands, his walk, his talk must have come into Christ's mind when he said the word 'father'. His mother, when they found him in Jerusalem, said, as mothers are inclined to do on such occasions, 'Your father and I …' Perhaps the bright young lad remembered it when he came twenty years on to tell the story of the Prodigal Son, observed and remembered the trick we play with relationships to claim or blame or plead. 'Your father and I …' said Mary; 'Your brother …' said the forgiving father; 'This son of yours …' said the angry brother. There wasn't much lost on the boy whom Joseph named Jesus.

The vision of the Father can only have come so easily to Christ because of his experience with Joseph. 'Your Father will reward you', 'Your Father who sees in secret', 'Your Father who knows what you want before you ask him', 'What man of you would give his son a stone if he asked for bread or a serpent if he asked for a fish or a scorpion if he asked for an egg?' Unthinkable if you knew Joseph. Who did Christ see when he asked, 'Who is the faithful and wise servant whom the master set over his household to give them their food?' and if he pitied the widow at Naim mourning her only son and saw his mother in her, then surely he thought of Joseph when he heard the man cry, 'Look upon my son for he is my only child' – and he gave him back his son. And above all I think we see Joseph in the love and wisdom and delight of the father of the prodigal son. We don't invent characters like that. We have to live with them. 'No one', as Christ said, 'knows the Father except the Son and anyone to whom the Son chooses to reveal him.'

Holy Thursday
This morning the Bishop used the Pope's letter on St John Vianney – his Holy Thursday letter – for his homily. St John Vianney is a man to be admired and the Pope admires him, the Bishop does, and I do. And I was glad to admire him again, and glad to have my attention drawn to him again, because long ago he endeared himself to me.

Often it is not what we admire people for that endears them to us. Often it is some minor thing, a phrase, a habit, a frailty that we like people for. And I remember St John Vianney with affection for one remark. Someone once said to him, 'And do you think it's all true?' The saint replied, 'If it isn't, I know one old man who's an awful fool.'

I suppose that's what a saint is – someone who's prepared to bet his life on it. It's not an easy bet. Everything you have goes on and there's no each way. But there's some endearing modesty, and some wry concession to doubting Thomas(es), in that 'If it isn't ...', much virtue in that 'if'. It keeps the saint human and within shouting – or at least praying – distance of the pack. A saint who's so far ahead he's out of sight would not be a good Holy Thursday saint for priests.

The Pope gave thanks for John Vianney on this feast of the Eucharist. We're not always aware enough that the Eucharist is a thanksgiving. A man was telling me the other day of a retreat he was at, where the priest made them write down their sins and then gathered the pages (foolscap but folded) and burned them. It might be an idea to write down – or even remember – the names of all the people you'd give thanks for in your life. It would be a long list I think – a real Book of Life. But then that's probably what the Book of Life is – the names of those for whom others including God give thanks, whose very existence is matter for thanksgiving, for Eucharist. 'My beloved Son in whom I am well pleased.'

There are so many to give thanks for – one's own people and one's friends, and the man who invented the electric light bulb and the wheel and the calculator. (That sounds as if he were the same man. In a way he is, I suppose. Whenever he comes along in history he invents something wonderful – *creator spiritus semper inveniens pro nobis* [we always find the Creator's spirit].) You have thanks to give for people who gave you a laugh yesterday and people who were reliable today and will be reliable next year. And people like Bob Geldof who have brilliant ideas and the will and the way to make them work. Thanksgiving like this is an enlargement of life. It draws in so many, such diverse people into one's Mass. The tens and tens of thousands at the Supper of the Lamb. And it skips over time and space. I give thanks for wisdom – for last year's scrap merchant who with no help rocked and turned and gently manoeuvred into his trailer a boiler section which it would have taken three men to lift. When I expressed wonder he said, 'Ah if you're nice to things they'll move for you.' I give thanks for the shared uncertainty that affects the teacher or writer – Ibn Battuta, I read in a magazine that arrived yesterday, was the greatest Muslim traveller of the Middle Ages. He wrote about Aleppo: 'Oh wonderful city! It endures but its owners have passed on. How many of its kings has it not changed into the past tense (expression borrowed from grammar)!' After six hundred years I sympathise with his parenthesis. I know that he wondered if the phrase would stand on its own or had he better explain it. And with sympathy, compassion and thanks I meet a fellow sufferer.

As priest and teacher I give thanks for and pray to be like the Dutch girl who died in Auschwitz in 1943 who wrote:

I embark on a slow voyage of exploration with everyone who comes to me ... And I thank You for the great gift of being able to read people. Sometimes they seem to me like houses with open doors. I walk in and roam through passages and rooms, and every house is furnished a little differently and yet they are all of them the same, and everyone must be turned into a dwelling dedicated to You, O God. And I promise You, yes I promise that I shall try to find a dwelling and a refuge for You in as many houses as possible ... There are so many empty houses and I shall prepare them all for You the most honoured lodger. Please forgive this poor metaphor.

'17 September',
Etty: The Letters and Diaries of Etty Hillesum, 1941–1943,
Etty Hillesum

With people like her one is already at the thanksgiving after Communion – and humble and grateful.

One could compose a Mass of litanies – a litany of failures, a litany of petitions, a litany of praises, a litany of gifts for the offertory, and a litany of thanksgivings. Above all, thanks – the Blessed Eucharist.

Good Friday
Even today's language casts a shadow. We easily say, 'Oh it's a crucifixion', about everyday darknesses and irritations. Maybe it trivialises but yet there's some sort of kinship. Writing and preaching are a kind of crucifixion – something I wish so much and so often I didn't have to do. People don't improve the pain by saying 'It came easy to you.' It's bad enough that it's not true but not to have the cost recognised doesn't help because we always like recognition for our pains. If no one is noticing we compel notice with a sigh (for bad form) or a pulled face (for toothache) or careful descent into a chair (for the back). That's for minor pains. When it's really bad we don't have to act. I think often of things Fr de Lubac said about suffering: 'When we really suffer we always suffer badly', 'No real suffering at the moment it is experienced is noble' and 'something will always be lacking to all suffering which has not been borne in solitude and secrecy. Even silence is not enough.'

But to each his own crucifixion. Mauriac said it was remarkable that two pieces of wood placed one upon the other should have assumed as many shapes as there are individual destinies. I thought of this again as the cross was carried round at the Stations. A crowded church and everyone there carrying a cross.

At the Fourth Station the priest read out that no mother ever suffered such sorrow. I don't know if what was meant was quantity or kind. I suppose it must mean quantity since so many mothers have seen sons die. I don't know how such terrible pain is measured, or how one can know if the statement is true. Anyway it puts the emphasis in the wrong place and the last thing the road to Calvary needs is a false step. The awful thing it seems to me is that Mary and so many millions like her have had to suffer helplessly by roadsides and bedsides – and the great thing is that Mary and her sisters and brothers have known the same sorrow. I remember once a woman telling me of how she felt angry when her eldest child had to emigrate – taken to America by relations. It was a great chance and they were poor – but the mother suffered bitterly. 'And then', she said, 'I thought of how God's mother felt over her own child. Even he couldn't spare her.' Two pieces of wood – but for some people they have roughly the same shape.

'The blows are struck, the blood gushes forth' – many people remember the set of prayers that were said at the Stations for years. Those were words used at the Eleventh Station. It's in some way symbolic that Christ who was a carpenter should have died by timber and hammer and nails – the tools of his trade. Died and yet found and gave new life. Our life work is the death of us and yet the life of us too. Through it we die, every day, and also find and give life. It seems true for priest, even more for parent. Parents seem to sacrifice so often and so much for their children – giving their today for their children's tomorrow, giving life through dying to themselves and yet finding life in their own emptying. When you think of homes in this way, one can only think that we live in the midst of great goodness and holiness.

2 April
This morning's paper has a headline, 'Vatican frees Father Boff.' I hadn't known they took prisoners in the Vatican now. Or was The *Independent* using liberation theology language?

The reference was to Fr Leonardo Boff and he is certainly different from the original Prisoner of the Vatican, Pius IX.

There are fashions in theology and spirituality as there are in literature – who's in, who's out, who's due for reassessment and temporary entombment, who's due for rediscovery and resurrection. The stones are always rolling – to close in or let out. Our designers are Roman or German or Dutch, and of late the Chicago collection has proved very popular. Indeed the adjectives used by the fashion writers can often describe the theological presentations – conservative, severe, romantic, revealing.

But it's very understandable. We are all Athenians at heart, always looking for something new – a new way of seeing, a new way of saying, a new way of praying, or a new appreciation of the old. Even in the realm of ideas we are pilgrim people always on the march, crossing another boundary, making for another horizon, always hungry for possession of further truth. I suppose it is really part of the fulfilment of Christ's promise of more abundant life.

But there is still regard for the old, and nothing gets lost. The Church throws very little out. Value is maintained and added. We may be at one moment stout Cortés seeing new oceans with wonder and thanks, but at another we are like David rediscovering an old sword with wonder and thanks, and saying like David 'Give me that, there is none like that.'

There are no sucked and discarded lemons. The zest remains. Spirit and memory, in Fr Shea's terms, are both essential parts of the encounter with God in Christ. No upper room ever devalues the stable. They are both rooms in the Father's mansion. But then the wise man brings out of his treasure new things and old.

> So let us now praise famous men –
> Noldin & Van Noort & Tanquerey;
> Schmaus, Ratzinger & also Rahner;
> Boff & Häring & all the Mcs.

Often they are hammer and anvil to one another, but the sparks that fly throw light, and the iron that is finally forged has the ring of truth.

5 April

Today a friend of mine showed me a report of a move by Quebec bishops to welcome 'divorcees, unmarried couples and single parent families into the Church'. We talked about it. I spoke with interest but he spoke with passion because he told me it affected his own family and he knew how good the people were and how much they longed to be fully at home again in the Church. It always gives new light when a daughter or brother or sister is involved. Law looks different when you can put the face and the name of one of your own on it.

(I met a woman the other day who was strongly against divorce. Twenty years ago I had heard her advocate it. When I reminded her of this she said, 'Oh maybe – but my children are married now and I see things differently. I think it will upset marriages.')

The report said resolutions were passed calling for 'an open door policy for families that don't fit the traditional model'. One woman who was a representative at the meeting said, 'There's going to be a reaction by people who feel very self-righteous, both among priests and parishioners.' That's war talk – you begin by tarring the opposition; put them among the Pharisees and they get automatic censure. But Christ didn't say all Samaritans were good and he didn't believe all Israelites were bad and he would have known goodness in some Pharisees too.

We often do less than justice to our neighbours and the truth by putting our fists up at the sign of disagreement. Once we assume an adversary position we seem to miss the others' goodness or pain. Sometimes those who don't see their way to doing something – such as allowing that people in irregular situations may receive the sacraments – are in greater agony than those who have no difficulty. It's too easy to throw in a word like 'self-righteous'. It doesn't advance causes. And I too must remember that no prayer the Church ever made said 'through your/his/her/their own fault', only '*mea culpa, mea culpa, mea maxima culpa*' (through my fault, through my fault, through my grievous fault). The apportioning of blame is not a major Christian task, but the recognition of one's own guilt is.

But it is still important to see the face, know the name, hear the voice even if it's at the edge of the crowd, or up a tree. It is when we recognise people that we are impelled to find a way. The way can be very hard to find. Perhaps this is because Christ is the way and he has a way of hiding himself – even or especially when we want to make him the wrong sort of king.

There are certainly many times in life when he's not easy to find. I can feel like Red Skelton's character Freddie the Freeloader, 'in whom', said his creator, 'there is a little bit of every one of you'. One of the things Red Skelton said of him was, 'He's never met God in person and he knows the next fellow just might be him.' Which brings me back to the woman who thinks the likes of me 'self-righteous'. Who is she? And could she be right?

Creator of Heaven and Earth

Vol. 41, No. 6, June 1980

There's a story told about Martin Luther – he was asked once what God did before he created the world, and Martin Luther replied that he was cutting canes for the people who were going to ask that question. The story, of course, says more about Martin Luther's humour than about God, but God would have been delighted with the answer because God delights in everything good, especially good humour. It would have delighted God too to see somebody made in his image making in his image. For, to our eyes and experience God is first and foremost a maker. 'Who made the world?' – the catechism's easiest question. 'God made the world' – the catechism's easiest answer.

We believe in God, the Creator of heaven and earth. That is the statement of our belief. It is easily and often made. It comes trippingly on the tongue. It slips by the mind, a phrase greased by years of use. It can be said with the brain in neutral. We have this habit of being casual with the momentous. We consort intimately, easily and thoughtlessly with infinity. The writers have noticed us, in wonder at our lack of wonder. John McGahern in one of his novels has somebody astonished at the Grace after Meals perfunctorily say: 'We give thee thanks, O Almighty God, for all thy benefits, who livest and reignest world without end. Amen' (*The Barracks*, John McGahern). 'World without end' – limitless vista – but we have our eyes on the empty plates and we only wonder whose turn it is to do the dishes.

But when you stop to think! We believe in God, the Creator of heaven and earth!

What does it mean when we stop to think? Different things to different people, of course. The theologian responds to one stimulus, the scientist to another but they will share too in the meanings and resonances of the phrase when it is prayed by all the faithful. 'Creator of heaven and earth' is a descriptive definition of God for us all. We define persons commonly by the work they do.

Who's Monsignor Horan? He's the man who built the airport. God is the Creator of heaven and earth, the world. The world was seen by writers through the ages as the *magnalia Dei*, God's great works. So the phrase begins by telling us about God from the evidence of Creation and it opens the door to wonder as we begin to think.

As we begin to think, we begin to marvel, because commonly when we think of heaven and earth, we move from sight to vision. We move from what we see in the everyday to a sort of cumulative vision of all Creation. We think of sky and clouds and stars, glory of sun and sheen of moon, mountains and snow, rivers and shining water, green fields and forests and flowers. The vision is of beauty and we look upon the earth as God must have looked on it in the first white days of the world. And we see that it is good – which is an original and spontaneous opinion every time it happens and one made of our own free will. It's very like a prayer. Indeed when it's properly written down it is a prayer.

> And you, sun and moon, O bless the Lord.
> And you, the stars of the heavens, O bless the Lord.
> And you, mountains and hills, O bless the Lord.
> And you, rivers and seas, O bless the Lord.

Works can move people to prayer, as people landing at Knock airport or meeting newly-arrived friends there will say: 'Well, God bless Monsignor Horan.'

Creeds have often had a bad reputation – dry and rigid and uncompromising – but the fault is so often in ourselves. We have named their parts as articles and spoken them grimly. 'Creator of heaven and earth' must be coloured by the gold of sunrise and the blaze of sunset and in that new light we may glimpse God coming on clouds of glory. So our descriptive definition moves easily from formal recognition to pleased prayer and the grey Creation of heaven and earth becomes God lit by the light he made. We begin to taste the juice and joy of Creation.

But as we pray the phrase, however quickly we say it, it bears still greater weight. Creator, as we all learned it, means the one who created out of nothing. We recognise briefly but radically, the difference between God and all other beings. In a seminary class hall or at a professor's desk this will rightly receive polysyllable expansion and distinction, but when we stand up in church or say the Creed as prelude to the rosary, we state our bare belief. We state it in a word – 'Creator' – but I think we see it as a picture with a positive and negative image each of which gives meaning to the other. The positive is ourselves – we can only make things out of things; we need iron, timber, thread, stone. The negative is God – we have not seen him at work, we have not seen it happen – but God is not like us. He creates – out of nothing. Behind the stone, behind the tree, there is God, not hiding but visible only in the negative. God is not us and not like us, though there are ways in which we are like God. We recognise a different being – totally, radically, essentially different from all the other beings. And we recognise there is, can be, only one such being – the Supreme Being. We believe in God. That's what the word 'Creator' says for us, God's people. It has the sense of the first statement in Christian literature of *creatio ex nihilo* (creation from nothing): 'God is one who created and established all things, bringing them into existence out of non-existence' (*The Shepherd of Hermas*).

'All things,' says the Shepherd. The Creed says 'heaven and earth'. It is the one bit of poetry in the sober statement and says more than *The Shepherd of Hermas*. 'All things' means what it says but it draws definite lines and inputs exact figures. One hundred per cent conveys the fact, but a one-dimension fact. The vastness of the immeasurable metaphor is more powerful here than mathematics. It is more satisfying for the mind that wants to express wonder and admiration and to give the gift of its faith. Gaelic has a way for saying 'everything' – *'Gach rud ó Neamh go hArainn'* ('everything from heaven to Aran'). It is a phrase that shares with the Creed the poetry of expansiveness, a generosity of expression that does not want to be exactly contained. We could count everything tediously on our fingers, but we haven't the meanness of mind for that and so in greatness of spirit we throw our arms wide and say 'heaven and earth'.

Again we have moved in inspiration of Spirit to prayer of praise and thanks, and refused to put any limits on what we offer except the limits God himself imposes on our vision – 'heaven and earth'. It's all his and we give credit where credit is due. Faith is a generous virtue. 'I believe' is not a phrase of the minimalist mind but a cry from the heart. Like Thomas's 'My Lord and My God.' 'Creator of heaven and earth' – no one could say more.

We have prayed the prayer of awe. It is an act of adoration. But it is not adoration of power, but of the goodness of God. We adore a Being that is beyond our understanding. We come to the beginning edge of infinity and we stop in awe. Our minds can go no further. 'Creator of heaven and earth.' We have no words left.

But 'earth' is our cue and God's. We come back to earth and God comes too. That's where we meet. God has a Word and the Word becomes flesh. So we continue 'and in Jesus Christ, his only Son, Our Lord'.

The progression Father-Creator-Son is every way right – logically and pedagogically. There is even a certain etymological rightness in it, since the Latin *creare* means 'to beget'. Christ is for the world and he is the meaning that the world seeks. The Father, the Creator, and his Creation, meet most perfectly in Jesus Christ, God and human. Jesus is the most perfect image of God in Creation. His relationship to the Father-Creator is the model of all our relationships – like Father, like Son, to coin a phrase. He and the Father are one and he does always the things that please the Father. In Christ there is perfect consonance of will and purpose between Creator and created. Jesus symbolises and is and achieves and will achieve the perfect reconciling of Creation and Creator. Christ is the summit of God's Creation and the revelation of God's purpose, 'his purpose which he set forth in Christ as a plan for the fullness of time, to unite all things in him, things in heaven and things on earth' (Eph 1:9, 10).

There is more to be said about Christ. Creation without Christ would lack its fullest meaning. Christ reveals to us the full meaning of our relationship to the Creator and to heaven and earth. He said he did not come to condemn the world but to save the world. The Lord of Salvation and the Lord of Creation are the same person. We begin to glimpse our own meaning as we see Christ's. For in the pattern of Christ we must not condemn the world, we must save the world.

'Creator of heaven and earth' immediately states a relationship between the Creator and Creation. It is first a relationship of origin and of responsibility but Genesis makes it a personal relationship and a relationship of delight. God saw all that he had made as good. He delighted in all that had being; he delighted in the shapes he had given, in the colours, in the meanings, in the possibilities. All those beings, light and people, water and animals, air and plants – they all participate in what God is. They are creatures – a word not to diminish their status by stressing their dependence, but a word first to tell their relationship with the Creator from whom they have received their being.

An American writer imagines God's delight in his Creation:

> From all eternity, it seems, he had this thing about being. He would keep thinking up all kinds of unnecessary things – new ways of being and new kind of beings to be. And, as they talked, God the Son suddenly said, 'Really, this is absolutely great stuff. Why don't I go out and mix us up a batch?' And God the Holy Ghost said, 'Terrific, I'll help you.' So they all pitched in, and after supper that night, the Son and the Holy Ghost put on this tremendous show of being for the Father. It was full of water and light and frogs; pine cones kept dropping all over the place and crazy fish swam round in the wine glasses. There were mushrooms and grapes, horseradishes and tigers – and men and women everywhere to taste them, to juggle them, to join them and to love them. And God the Father looked at the whole wild party and said 'Wonderful! Just what I had in mind.'

> *The Third Peacock*,
> Robert Farrar Capon

So the basis for our emerging awareness of the relationship of all being, the interdependence of all forms of being, is in the faith we profess in the Creed. To believe in God the Creator of heaven and earth is to accept God's revelation of his care and his love for Creation and to accept the responsibility of being God's image as we care for and love all God made.

Sin enters the world as the opposite of God's will for his creatures – when thinking creatures misuse part of God's Creation. It may be one of his creatures from the world of the numinous who takes the form of a serpent and misleads two human beings. It may be two human beings who take fruit from the wrong tree. It may be a generation of human beings who destroy the wrong trees in Brazil or Africa. It may be an army of human beings who defoliate trees with Agent Orange. Or it may be just the simple ordinary everyday hurt that one of us can do to another. We are slowly coming to appreciate that 'Creator of heaven and earth' means that we – all Creation – participate in the being of the one who *is* Being, and so by our very nature and design we affect one another. We, all things, are married to one another for better or for worse, and this marriage was made in heaven, and not even death does us part. If anybody gets hurt everybody gets hurt. We are in this together.

God gives existence, gives life out of love. This love holds all things in being at every moment. So when we say 'Creator of heaven and earth' we are talking about now and we are talking about love. We are not looking back in wonder but looking around us. We see created sheep in created fields, created flowers waving to created air in created grass, and created people collaborating with or resisting their Creator. God is at work now. We do not see the hand but we see the handiwork. To realise this immanent power of God in all things gives a new meaning to life. Even when we walk or talk we do so through the dynamic presence of the Creator of heaven and earth. And this immediacy of God can lead to an intimacy with God. Creation can become, as the old writers saw it, a *paidagogos* (tutor or slave to young boy) – leading us to the Creator as one might take a child by the hand to school.

In being led to the Creator we are being led to our own meaning, at least to an assurance that we matter. 'Creator of heaven and earth' dots the 'i', it will take Christ to cross the 't'. But the dotted 'i' is its own letter. I matter because I matter to my Creator. 'Without the Creator the creature would disappear. When God is forgotten the creature itself grows unintelligible,' says Vatican II's *Gaudium et Spes*. But the Creed is the remembering of God and when we remember and say 'Creator of heaven and earth', then we confer intelligibility on ourselves. The Creator rescues us from absurdity. Sartre said once, 'Everything that exists is born for no purpose, continues through weakness, dies by chance' (*Being and Nothingness*, J.P. Sartre). When we affirm belief in the Creator we contradict the absurd, for we believe we know whom we come from and through whom we continue and to whom we go. And we affirm our purpose because we believe in a Creator who cares and we believe in Einstein's phrase that 'God does not play dice with the Universe.' When King Edwin of Northumbria sat at York and wondered with his counsellors whether to become a Christian, one of them told a famous fable. Life, he said, was like a sparrow flying out of the winter darkness into the firelight of a hall and then after a moment of warmth and safety, flying out into the night again. 'So this life of man', he said, 'appears for a short space but of what went before or of what is to follow we are utterly ignorant.' Perhaps this story is an earlier version of Sartre or maybe it has no overtones of hopelessness and is just a statement of fact, still valid in its way. For dark there is before our beginning and after our death, but now it is an inhabited dark. It is dark inhabited by the Creator of heaven and earth and that dark is light enough. We are no longer afraid of what's there because we know who's there.

The Creator confers intelligibility and meaning on creatures. The human being, who participates most fully of the beings of the earth in being itself, has a unique meaning on the created earth. 'We alone know that we know.' 'We are both distinct from nature and at one with nature in that we too are part of the whole created order' (*Catholicism*, Richard P. McBrien, p. 225).

The human being is made in the image of God, a being to appreciate, to collaborate, to make, indeed, in a sense, to create, and a being free to choose to do or not to do any of these actions. The rest of earth's Creation will obey perfectly the will of the Creator. Every beaded bubble winking at the brim is perfectly what it should be in shape and place and colour, as it reflects light, as it bursts. But it cannot speak. It cannot choose. It cannot delight in. In this inability it resembles all the other beings of earth except human beings.

We are the voice of Creation, able to acknowledge, to give thanks, to praise, to proclaim 'Creator of heaven and earth'. God said, 'I have made you like gods.' And so we share in divine characteristics. Outside us is a world and a universe whose size and complexity we may be able to state but which we cannot comprehend, indeed which is not even fully imaginable for us. If I am told that light travels at 186,000 miles per second and that we are eight light minutes from the sun – this I can imagine. When I'm told that the galaxy of which we are part is 100,000 light years across – I can state it but I cannot imagine it. If you tell me there are maybe some hundred thousand million galaxies each containing some hundred thousand million stars – I can really express it only mathematically, and not only can I not imagine it but my imagination boggles at even considering the task. Then I read that the number of bits of information built into one human being is a number one million times greater than the number of all the stars in the universe.

The human being inhabits an awesome world – outside him is mathematically huge and imaginatively almost infinite; inside him, to an even greater mathematical reality, an imaginatively impossible figure. The human being stands between the two – the discoverer of both in their immensity and complexity. We are the thin waist of the hourglass between the macrocosm and the microcosm. In us they meet, through us the prayer of the whirling spheres and the whirling particles must go back to the Creator of heaven and earth. We are the priests of Creation.

We are like the Creator when we delight in the marvel of Creation, when we are driven to wonder at the Creator whose work beggars our imagination. We are like our Creator too when we create, in partnership with our Creator. 'Every good action comes from God as well as the doer.' Together as primary cause and secondary cause they create goodness. It might be a smile or a word or a deed, but it brings into being goodness which did not exist before. It gives a new shape to time. It stamps a segment of time with the seal of God and of a human. Together God and a human have marked 'Saved' on a sequence of time, which could have been wasted or even damaged and lost. It is when collaboration becomes creation that we realise the full meaning of Irenaeus's phrase, 'The glory of God is the human being fully alive.' It is at such moments that the hand of the Creator finally grasps the hand of Adam and they walk together again.

There are other moments. There have been many, when we walk away and go it alone. We have, in Yeats's words, danced drearily 'to the cracked tune that Chronos sings' ('The Song of the Happy Shepherd', W. B. Yeats). We have refused to join the harmony of the eternal, and God permits us to choose and follow our own way even though it is a *reductio ad absurdum* (reduction to absurdity).

Christ came to restore the broken harmony. He does it, of course, by being himself the perfection of Creation, the divine and the human in one person. But this person enacts and achieves the reconciliation by doing everything in union with, in thanks for, in praise of, the Father. And that is our final reconciled destiny too – to praise God. Our acknowledgement in the Creed, 'Creator of heaven and earth', is a foreword to heaven. The Sanctus expands it, 'Holy, Holy, Holy Lord, God of power and might. Heaven and earth are full of your glory, Hosannah.'

That's the way the angels and saints put it. Rilke puts it in his own way:

I praise.	But the deadly and the monstrous things,
	how can you hear them?
I praise.	But what is nameless, what is anonymous,
	how can you call upon it?
I praise.	What right have you to be true in every disguise,
	behind every mask?
I praise.	How is it that the calm and violent things like star
	and storm know you for their own?
Because I praise.	

'Creator of heaven and earth' is a prayer of praise, in which we become priest to the Creator, priest for Creation.

There is one other twentieth-century area for which the phrase 'Creator of heaven and earth' poses a question and challenge. Scientists, physicists, mathematicians every day reach farther back or deeper in or higher up to discover the origin of the universe or the complete theory which would explain and describe the universe. *Gaudium et Spes* gives a lively blessing to their efforts:

Earthly matters and the concerns of faith derive from the same God. Indeed whoever labours to penetrate the secrets of reality with a humble and steady mind, is, even unawares, being led by the hand of God, who holds all things in existence and gives them their identity.

'Being led by the hand of God.' We are back at the *paidagogos*. Being led where? Stephen Hawking, the renowned theoretical physicist, makes an interesting comment on the *terminus ad quem* (finishing point) in the last paragraph of his book *A Brief History of Time*. He says that,

If we do discover a complete theory of how the universe works ... then we shall all, philosophers and scientists and just ordinary people, be able to take part in the discussion of the question of why it is that we and the universe exist. If we find the answer to that, it would be the ultimate triumph of human reason – for then we would know the mind of God.

Reason is one of the lights we let play on 'the Creator of heaven and earth' to know more about him and his work, and to feed our faith and our prayer. But imagination has its place too. The poets have as much to say as the scientists or philosophers. Indeed they need one another because the search for the full glory and the full meaning needs all hands. One can almost wonder which discipline one is engaged in when one learns from a scientist about the varieties of quark – the particles which make up protons and neutrons and electrons. Stephen Hawking says 'there are thought to be at least six "flavours" which we call up, down, strange, charmed, bottom and top. Each flavour comes in three "colours", red, green and blue.' And the very word 'quark' comes from a quotation from James Joyce. 'Three quarks for Muster Mark' – which sounds suspiciously like something being said in a North of Ireland accent. The labour to 'penetrate the secrets of reality' needs all sorts of collaborations. As James Joyce might say, 'Here comes Everyman.' But we shouldn't wonder because the object of our odyssey is the Creator of heaven and earth, the Creator of us all.

The scientist's task may seem very different from Everyman and Everywoman standing in church to say 'I believe in God … the Creator of heaven and earth.' *Time* magazine has a cartoon of a scientist with a butterfly net chasing particles. But the search for the elementary constituents of matter and the acknowledgement of the Ground of our Being are together part of our common walk to the World's Second Communion. Prayer uses its own particles – bread and wine and water and oil and salt – to search for God and for reconciliation with the Creator and harmony with Creation. The prayer of faith, says St James, will save the sick man. Our prayer of faith in the Creed is more than a statement of adherence. 'Creator of heaven and earth' are healing words too and words of hope. As we say them we know that we stand in the great hand of God, the infinitely gentle and infinitely caring. So the next line of the Creed should be no surprise – 'And in Jesus Christ.' Incarnation seems only natural for a God who loves so much.

God and the Ugly Duckling
– *A Homily on Baptism*
Vol. 43, No. 1, January 1992

I want to tell you a story. There once was an ugly duckling. But maybe you'll say – 'but I know that story and anyway I thought I was going to hear about baptism and new life in Christ.' Well, there's a connection. That's an important word, and I'd like to talk about connections too, not the electrical sort, but the Irish sort – you know, 'the relations', what you hear at weddings: 'didn't she get a grand fellow? And he's very well connected, I believe', or at a funeral: 'what are you doing here?' – 'Oh she's a connection of our own.' Connections are very important.

But let me come back to the ugly duckling. You remember the famous story. The duck hatches out her eggs and she has lovely fluffy yellow ducklings – all except one that came from a very big egg, and this one is a big awkward bird and all the others laugh at it. The ducks laugh at it, it can't quack; the hens laugh at it, it can't cluck; the cats laugh at it, it can't purr. They call it the ugly duckling. Nobody wants it; it has no friends. It's an outcast, and when winter comes it can stand no more of the mockery and it goes off to live alone in the woods.

But ugly as it is, it has dreams. One day it sees big white birds flying gracefully across the sky and it thinks, 'If only, if only I could be like that.' It was only a dream, of course. The ugly duckling had no hope of it ever happening. Then one winter, cold and alone, this frustrated ugly duckling sees three of the great white birds sailing majestically on the lake. And, wonder of wonders, the three swans – for that's what they were – swam over and said to the ugly duckling, 'Come and join us.' But he says, 'I couldn't. I'm only an ugly duckling. I have no friends and I'm no use. Please kill me and put me out of pain.' And the three swans say, 'What do you mean "no use"? You are beautiful and you are one of us. Look at yourself

– ⌒ 41 ⌒ –

in the water.' And the ugly duckling looked in the mirror water and saw himself for the first time as he really was – graceful, white, beautiful. He said, 'Is that really me?' and they said, 'Of course it is.' 'But,' he said, 'I look like you – what am I?' 'You're a swan,' they said, 'come and join us.' And his heart beat very fast with excitement and he was so happy that he almost did not dare breathe.

Do you think you'd ever look at yourself in wonder like that and ask, 'What am I?' and hear a voice which says, 'You're one of us, come and join us'? And would your heart beat very fast with excitement and would you be so happy that you almost would not dare breathe? Anyway, you don't, I dare say, and I know I don't and yet if we *really* understood our baptism, if we *really* looked into the water of baptism and saw who we *really* are, we would give thanks with beating heart and breathlessly. For that's the first meaning of baptism. It's the voice of God saying, 'You're one of us; you're made in my image. You look like me. You're not an ugly duckling. You're a swan. I love you. Come and join us.'

Our baptism is an ugly duckling story, a rags to riches, a Cinderella story but it is one that began in the imagination of God and it happened. God's dreams all come true. Indeed we were outcasts – cast out of the garden of our dreams, in an exile subject to pain and disease and unease and broken promises and broken friendships, where life is lived under the shadow of death. The swans may fly high in summer but the human race lives like the ugly duckling, in a wintry world with a sorry history.

It's a world where we mean well and our meanings go astray, a world where we promise and mean to keep our promises and fail not once but again and again. It's a world where the young have hopes that the old know won't happen because they know how life gets sour and how what started out as poetry so often finishes as prose. And what disturbs is not so much the failure as the lack of fulfilment.

But each of us knows too, senses, that it might have been different, could be different. Each of us knows too that there is more good in us than ever comes to the surface, that there is more to us than ever appears, if only, if only it could be released. The swans fly across the sky – somehow we know we could have flown if only … If only what? If only things were right – but they never were.

Will they ever be? Must the ugly duckling remain an ugly duckling forever? Is there hope? Or is death the only remedy for life?

And the three swans came sailing majestically across the water and said, 'Come and join us.' Baptism is the sacrament of hope, the foundation of all our hope. It is the sacrament of new life for it is the sacrament that contradicts death. It gives not just new life to us but new meaning to all we do. Christ takes the doom of 'if only' out of our dreams and makes the dream come true. Baptism is all that. But it begins as a sacrament of welcome, welcome home. Come and join us.

It's like going into a house where there are people sitting round a fire, and their backs are towards you and then someone sees you and says, 'Oh, you're welcome. Get a chair, pull out there and let him in' and chairs are pulled and the circle is enlarged and you are brought into the company and the light and the warmth and the friendship, welcome and made at home. Baptism is like that – God's arms out to welcome us into the family of God, into the light and love and life of the three persons, the Father, the Son and the Holy Spirit. 'Come on in,' says God, 'make yourself at home; this place wouldn't be the same without you.' And God means every word of it. So baptism is the end of exile, it is also the beginning of a new life, a new person, a new identity.

It was only when the ugly duckling looked in the water that he saw himself in all his reality and possibility. It is only when we look into the water of baptism that we see who we really are, see the person God loves and dreams of – the possible you, not the impossible you – the possible you, meant for eternity, the you who can reflect God, you kind, you forgiving, you generous, you merciful, you thanking. 'Come and join us,' said the three swans, 'you're one of us.' But you'll say like the duckling, 'That's not me. Is that me?' You'll think, 'Ah, you don't know me, the real me, the mean me, complaining me, intolerant, unforgiving, unloving, impossible me.' But will you look in the water and reflect on your reflection, your baptismal reflection, brother, sister of Jesus Christ?

We don't look, however. We forget, and forgetting we find ourselves reduced to the smallness of the isolated self. And when we forget baptism and who we are, then we have a greater sense of prison than of freedom, greater sense of failure than of success, greater sense of distress than of hope. We live like ugly ducklings in the winter woods.

But Christ is a summer Christ and baptism is a sacrament of flowing water, not frozen water. Christ came to take the chill out of our relationship with God, to warm Adam's chapped hands and to take Eve's cold hands in his. He is a summer Christ – in wonder at the generosity of the widow, delighted by the wit of the woman who said even the dogs get the crumbs, astounded at the faith of a Roman soldier, teasing Martha, rejoicing in Mary. He's a Christ who loves children, and cries with the heartbroken. A Christ who's not interested in our sins except to forgive them, and who paints the forgiveness of God as three happy faces – a man who got his sheep back, a woman who got her money back and a father who got his son back. He pities hunger and feeds it, he pities fear and calms it. His face is not icy or dark or threatening – it's warm and bright and inviting. Christ brought back the summer.

And his followers, the baptised? Would you know us out of him? By our brightness? By our hope? By our delight in the good? There was a famous atheist who said he couldn't believe because Christians looked so unredeemed. One of the old saints – St Leo the Great – once preached a famous sermon which said: 'Recognise, O Christian, your nobility. It is God's own nature you share.' He was really saying: 'Remember what your baptism means – remember who you are. Look in the water and see yourself.' God has called us, as the Sunday Preface says, 'to the glory that has made us a chosen race, a royal priesthood, a holy nation, a people set apart'. 'The Son of God,' says St Augustine, 'was made the Son of Man, so that the sons and daughters of men would become the sons and daughters of God.' It must puzzle God that we so often think so little of ourselves.

'Come and join us,' God says. We hear the words and we miss the meaning. Christ comes in baptism to draw us to our full height – a chosen race, a people set apart. But our souls stay small – poor relations with the poor mouth. And we miss all the juice and joy of baptism. We hear that baptism is new life in Christ, and we feel it's something good without being sure what.

But Christ never says anything that isn't full of meaning. He was the Word of God, and the Word became flesh not to waste words but to give words meaning – to take the word 'life' and stretch it to eternity, to take the word 'love' and stretch it to infinity. Christ came to give us new life. 'Come and join us – you're one of us.' Look at the company we travel in. We're very well connected.

So we're here this evening with the weight of the world on us – but not maybe the way you think. Oh, many of us may have come here heavily burdened, suffering deeply with pain of body or mind or spirit, at our wits' end or the end of our tethers, in the desperation that ill-health or unemployment or weather or worry or stock or love or land or children can bring us to. That weight of the world may be on us and we'll pray together for God's help for that.

But there's another weight and it's the weight of the world on God. God has his troubles too and he needs our help. He sent Christ, of course, to save the world, but he sent him to get help too. And here we are, God's help, God's baptised people. So many things we'll do or pray will happen, we say, 'with God's help'. Who is God's help? Here we are.

You see, when we live our baptism we change the world. Everything's different. We take the fear out of death. We're no longer afraid of what's beyond the grave, because we know who's beyond the grave – a connection of our own, and sure, there's favour in heaven. We take the fear out of life. We're no longer afraid of life because we're strong in the strength of Father, Son and Holy Spirit. Like St Patrick we bind unto ourselves this day the strong name of the Trinity.

And we need that strength, because this is a world which has little time for the ugly duckling. The standards or ways of Christ find little favour among those who set the glitzy, ritzy fashions of the day. And Christians will often feel isolated and maybe a little foolish, standing for things that are ridiculed as out of date, unenlightened, foolish, Victorian, obscurantist, antediluvian – there's no shortage of belittling words. It isn't always easy to have firm faith when you're being pitied for your ignorance or laughed at for your stupidity. The hens still smirk at the ugly duckling who can't cluck, the cats still mock because he can't purr. All he can do is swim and, as the hens said, 'Swim! And, my dear, who wants to?'

So if our faith and hope are to remain firm and confident we must look in the water. 'Who am I?' said the ugly duckling. 'You're one of us,' said the three. 'What am I?' said he. 'You're a swan,' said they. 'Can this really be me?' said he, 'I look like you.' And they said, 'Of course it's you. Come and join us.' And together they swam away, the three and the one they had made one of them.

And you were baptised in the name of the Father and of the Son, and of the Holy Spirit, the three persons of the Trinity.

May the life you were given by the flowing water grow stronger each day in you, until that day when it reaches the fullness of its promise in that land to which the swans fly to eternal summer.

Hope and the Hungers of the Heart

Vol. 43, No. 10, October 1992

I want to begin with a question and a story. The question is: Do you know what bullseyes are? They're hard sweets you suck – striped black and white – a bit like life, but sweeter. Sometimes, anyway. That's the question, and I'll come back later to the bullseyes. The story is a personal one. A few years ago I met a woman who told me about an old man she had met fifty years before. The old man told her about his wife who had died forty years before that, a young woman, leaving him with four young children. She said as he talked about his life he began to cry – still lonely for her and, he said, looking forward to meeting her soon in heaven. Well, the man was my grandfather and I thought of him tonight because I am preaching about what made him cry – hope and the hungers of the heart. And I thought of this particularly this night, for my grandmother – the young woman who died – had been a teacher here in Knock and actually gave evidence before the commission investigating apparitions at Knock. And this night is the night the apparition took place. So that's the story, a Knock story in a way, about hope and the hungers of the heart. By the way, the commission said about my grandmother that her face was so honest you would have to believe her – so now you know where I got it from.

But to come back to the bullseyes. At the end of Frank O'Connor's story about the young lad making his First Confession, the young lad comes out to his waiting older sister, Nora, and she says to him, 'What are you sucking?'
'Bullseyes.'
'Was it the priest gave them to you?' she said.
''Twas,' he said.
And Nora says, 'Almighty God, some people have all the luck. I might as well be a sinner like you, there's no use in being good.'

Did you ever get tired of being good? I mean a bit fed up of praying and trying to do the right thing, and telling the children the right thing, and doing your best, and doing novenas? Did you ever get fed up of it, tired of trying and nobody paying any attention to you – not even God? And you'd get fed up of God too. And you don't say it to anyone but feel it – feel that faith and hope have leaked out and your heart is dry, and weary and going nowhere. And it isn't that you want to do anything wicked, not really wicked, only – maybe – you want to kick off your shoes, and toss your head, and stop worrying about money, and work and this to do today, and that to do tomorrow. Stop the world, I want to get off and be different. The people who don't care at all seem to be better off. 'I might as well be a sinner. There's no use in being good.' Who gets the bullseyes?

Did you ever feel like that? Your heart hungry to be different – wanting life and not getting it, looking for magic poetry and getting mashed potatoes – and where's the gravy? They're too dry. Oh, indeed, where's the gravy? If you ever felt like that you'll feel for the woman who wrote: 'When I am an old woman I shall wear purple with a red hat which doesn't go, and doesn't suit me. And I shall spend my pension on brandy and satin sandals and say we have no money for butter. I shall sit down on the pavement when I am tired and gobble up samples in shops, and I'll go out in my slippers in the rain and I'll learn to spit.'

'I'll learn to spit' – not everybody's ambition maybe, but you know what she meant; even more, you know how she felt. Her heart was crying out for another life, for more life. Where's the gravy? And where's God? Would you if you got the chance have something to say to him? Even something as short as the little girl I knew once? She was only eight or nine but she had a problem with her prayers and her parents asked me to chat to her about it. Well, I asked her did she pray and she said 'No.' And I said, 'Do you talk to God?' She said, 'Oh I do.' And I said, 'And what do you say to him?' She said, 'I say "Shut up, you".' Shut up, you – would we say it if we dared? So we say it behind clenched teeth, when we need God and God is there only, it seems, through restrictions – a negative and negating God, and there's no gravy.

Oh we go to confessions and we accuse ourselves. We have offended God. We're the defendants, God is the plaintiff. We admit, we confess, and we beat our breasts, 'through my fault, through my fault, through my most grievous fault'. We confess but in the court of the heart who stands accused? Are we plaintiff and is God defendant, when we bring our case against him? 'Look what you did to us. You stood and looked on' – and the chorus of human recriminations would rise to high heaven: for my sister who died young; for the husband I lost tragically; for the child who died before birth; for my brother's pain and he doesn't deserve it; for the misery of my marriage and it's not my fault; for the work I cannot get and I need it; for the fighting, the poverty, for the hunger, the injustice, for the loneliness; for the love that I lost and the love that turned to hate and the love that went dull, and the love that just gave up and died. 'God, don't you realise you have offended us? You could have done something about it and you did nothing.' And God doesn't answer. God stays silent.

Are we like the old woodcutter who got a bit drunk and lost his way home in the forest and lay down and fell and found himself taken before God for judgement? And the angels wouldn't talk to him and God was cross with him – said he drank too much and went home too late and cheated his customers and he'd have to carry a block of wood on his back for punishment. And the woodcutter suddenly said, 'No, I won't. I haven't done half the things to you that you did to me. You left me without a father and my mother died young. I have to cheat because I am so poor and I'd starve if I did not. My wife abuses me and the ribs on my horse stick out like fence posts. I'll carry no block of wood for you.' And the story says the angels stood in horror at this cheek to God. And God? God started crying and said, 'I never knew it was like that, I am sorry. How can I make it up to you? You can stay here and everything will be all right, or if you prefer you can go back and give it another go.' And the woodcutter said he would go back and try this life again. And God said, 'Good man yourself.' So he woke up in the forest, feeling all right and happy with himself and he got to his hut and went in. And immediately his wife rushed at him and hit him with the pan and abused him for a drunken sod that was never home in time and all the woodcutter did was look up to heaven and shake his head. He had gone home with hope and here he was as bad as ever. Almost, not quite. For at least now he felt somebody saw and noticed and understood.

Well that's only a story. But this isn't. Long ago God sent, not a woodcutter exactly, but a carpenter, a carpenter who was a very good carpenter and did not cheat at all and did God's will as perfectly as possible. And one day we put a block of wood on his shoulders and we knocked him and we abused him and so he couldn't get free of the wood. We nailed him to it, so that he'd be there for all time. And then we mocked him and said: 'Where's your God now? You said he was your Father. If he is, let him come now and take you down.' But the Father never came and the carpenter died. And just before he died he said, as we say so often, 'Where are you, God? Why have you forsaken me?' He said that, the carpenter, and then he said what we find it hard to say, and I suppose he found it hard to say too. He said, 'Father, into your hands I commend my spirit.' He said, 'I don't see you, I don't hear you, but I know you see me, and you hear me and I know you love me, so I trust you.' And the story didn't end there. For what do you think happened? Didn't the carpenter rise from the dead and the block of wood was gone and the pain was gone and he was all he ever could be – a new person? Just what we long to be – me and you and that woman who wants to wear purple with a red hat.

So where are we now? The story of the woodcutter – the story that's only a story – tells us how we feel it is sometimes. But the story of the carpenter – the story that's not just a story but real – tells us how it is always, whether we feel it or not. In the story that's only a story we look up to heaven and we do the talking and there's no answer, only more of the same, the same old life. In the story that is true, heaven looks down on us and says: 'I know how you feel and I see and I hear and I sent you an answer – oh and not just in words. I gave you my Word. I sent you my Son. He's my answer. I hope you find him satisfactory. I was well pleased with him.'

So now we face a different question. Is Christ a satisfactory answer to the questions we have for God? When the heart is hungry, is there any hope for us in Christ? We need to know, for we are the people St Paul talks of who have put our hope in Christ. We are the people who say we wait in joyful hope for the coming of Our Saviour Jesus Christ. So will he come, this Christ?

Well, he promised.

Yes but will he live up to his promise? We are so used to broken promises in our world, you might think another one would not surprise us – but this one would drive us to despair. So will he come, this Christ? Will he be there when we need him? Well, he says 'always'. 'Always', he says, until the end of the world. Ah, but can you believe him?

Well, he promised.

But promises are cheap.

Sometimes. This one was dear. It cost him his life.

So can Christ live up to his promises? He knows the pain and he pitied it on earth – pitied Martha's grief and gave her back Lazarus, pitied Jairus and gave him back his little daughter, pitied the widow at Naim and gave her back her only son. But where is this Christ now?

He pitied them. Does he pity us too? Oh, pity us, Christ, and while we are waiting, pity us now.

Now – isn't that when we want help? Now. Even when we accept the promise of the future, the promise of eternal life and meeting again all those we love – even when we accept that, we want help and hope for now. The Jews have a prayer, 'God will help me, but oh that he helps me, until he helps me.' We mightn't have the words for that song, but we all know the air. We need God's help now. And he said, 'Come to me all you who are weary and heavily burdened and I will refresh you.' Lord, we are here. We need help now.

Why doesn't Christ help us as he helped the people he met in Palestine? We could fairly say we know him better than they. We've talked to him long hours, committed ourselves to him and his kingdom. Why wouldn't he do for us what he did for them? Had the little girl in the story the right of it? Almighty God, some people have all the luck. What's the use of being good at all? It remains a question – trivially put, but seriously meant. We could come to no better place for an answer than to Knock, *Cnoc Mhuire*, Mary's place.

Jesus gave Lazarus back to Martha and a young man back to his mother. He didn't give Joseph back to Mary. Did Mary deserve less? He changed water into wine when she asked. Could he not have changed death into life when she wept? And she was full of grace. What's the use of being good at all?

I think Mary makes us realise we are asking the wrong question. It doesn't have to do with being good, not ever. Christ raised Lazarus, cured the woman, calmed the troubled waters, but Lazarus died again some day and Jairus's little skipping daughter grew up, grew old and died again, and the water in the lake of Galilee has risen in many a storm since, and the wind has roared again. You see, all these miracles were only signs, not solutions. They were signs of God's care and God's power, but the solution, the answer to our prayers and tears and to Mary's tears and prayers was Christ, who died and rose again, and who is, as St Paul says, only the first to go where we will follow.

Christ is God's answer and Mary is Christ's. Oh, it's now we need our resurrections, but Christ did not give Joseph back to Mary. Not then. Mary had to wait, like my grandfather. This world is a waiting room and Mary's time in that room gives meaning to ours. For as Christ tells us through Mary, he did not come to take away the pain from this world, he came to give it meaning. Just as Mary stood at the foot of his Cross, her grief going to God like a prayer, through Christ, so all who stand on Calvary are part of the force which gives new life to the world. We become God's carpenters, other Christs, people who make the world better with their hands, with their care, with their prayers and with their offered pain, the strongest prayer of all.

Our questioning of God fades as we come close to Jesus and Mary, for with them we become part of the answer. We drink from the same cup, we are part of the family. Like Christ and Mary we are wounded healers. Only Christ in all human history made wounds other than wounds, and death other than death.

For his strong promise is that our wounds are for the healing of the world now and they are a prayer as long as this world will last, and death is simply the door to the life, the fuller greater life our heart longs for, the life God made us for.

Do you remember how he proved himself to Thomas? 'Look at my wounds' – his sign. His hands bear the marks still, a prayer before God for us all, and a sign, a statement that he will never forget us, and that he is one with all those who bear the marks. He is one with the fallen, for he fell, one with the weeping, for he wept, one with the beaten, for he failed. There is nothing in the vast history of human suffering that he does not take to himself – he came to be one of us, to stamp our time with love, and light our pain with meaning and hope. Oh, but what about those who had no hope, who could no longer face this life, the men and the women, the boys, the girls whose hope ran out and who in despair or anger or frustration took their own lives? Did the light Christ came to give and to be fail for them? Oh no. The old prayer said: 'Blessed be God who has placed hope in the grave.' God waited for them on the other side of their despair – that God who understood so well the darkness of feeling forsaken, and alone and helpless, that God who cried out in the garden as the terror he faced became unbearable. Christ's cry in the garden, says Pope John Paul, is the cry of the human being in anguish, faced with what he may not be able for. So Christ knew the despair and the terror. Every Gethsemane is his garden. The Irish prayer put it another way: 'He is the king of the Friday and we are *all* his people.'

So he is our hope for the restless part of us that hungers for more life. His Resurrection is the promise for us now of that new life we crave. He is hope now for the heart, hungry for lost love, lost peace, lost health – for he gives meaning to our loss, as he partners us in it and makes our pain a prayer, shared pain and shared prayer. He is our hope, but not only that, he makes us the hope of others. He gives us the power of being hope to one another – now. Christ came to be one of us and so to feel for us – so that we'd know God knew what was happening at the ends of our nerves and in the fibres of our beings. But Christ came too to make sense of the absurdity of life, to make grace of the obscenity of suffering, to give meaning and purpose to the hunger of the heart. He came to empower us as God's hope for this time and for this place – 1992 on Planet Earth.

There is an old belief that Christ will stay on his Cross until every person in the world agrees to take him down. We're a long way from agreement and so Christ stays on his Cross in Sarajevo and Somalia, and places nearer home, and in small rooms and houses that give no sign of it, and in hearts that hide their break. Christ is in agony until the end of the world and we must not rest during that time. We hungry hearts must ourselves become the world's hope. For that, God brings us to Knock so that in Mary's place we may, like her, discover the part God has given us to play in the drama of this world – not just supporting players, not just bit players, but understudies to the Son of God. An understudy takes over when the actor cannot be there. And since Christ's away, Christ must play, night and day, in ten thousand places, through us. We're to speak his words, we are to imitate his actions, we are to think his way. 'Let that mind be in you', says St Paul, 'which was also in Christ Jesus.'

So we are God's hope, we with our depressions, and our illnesses and our griefs and our worries. We are God's hope. We wonder at times, 'where will I turn?' – and when there is no one else we will turn to Padre Pio, or St Jude or St Anthony, or to Mary or to Christ. We turn to them, God turns to us. 'Where will I turn?' thinks God. 'I'll turn to Mick, or Pat would do; there's always Betty, and Nora never lets me down.' That's our closeness with God, and it gives strength and meaning to us now, and glory after, when God thanks us for the times he turned to us.

That's why we're ready to greet Christ when he comes again, that's why we call out at the consecration, 'Christ has died, Christ has risen, Christ will come again.' For Christ made all the difference in the world – he makes the hunger of our hearts the hope of our heaven. So why wouldn't we be glad to see him and wait indeed in joyful hope?

The Irish word for 'and' is *agus* and there's an Irish word for a bit you tack on to something that you say – it's called an *aguisín*. I just want to add one *aguisín*. There's an old Connaught Prayer for all sinners – *na daoine a bhíonn go síorraí ag dul ar strae,* the people that are always going astray. And this prayer says: Ah, but they're Mary's people. Isn't she praying for us sinners always, and so when we go before God for Judgement

> Mary will go on her bended knees
> In front of her Son Divine,
> Saying 'Remember the promise you made me
> When we lived in Palestine.'
> And he'll say 'I remember, Mother,
> And every word of it's true,
> The people you pray for, that your mantle wear,
> Will live here with me and you.'

It was that hope and that faith that made the Irish give a blessing to people, *Faoi bhrat Mhuire thú*, may you be under Mary's mantle, in the protection of her who is our life, our sweetness and our hope. Mary's mantle is our cape of good hope.

So may you leave Knock tonight with new hope, as those who saw Mary did on this night long ago. New hope in the meaning of your life now, and new hope for the future, the glorious future God has prepared for you.

Faoi bhrat Mhuire sibh go léir.
May the mantle of Mary enfold you and yours always.

As I See It
– Holy Week Meditations
Vol. 44, No. 4, April 1993

My name's Peter

He gave me the name himself – the very first Christian name. It means rock, steady as a rock. Oh I remember this week, I remember it well. People talk about being up at cockcrow – I used to redden at the word. I even hated bright mornings; I felt every cock in Creation knew about it. Well, I let down the Creator – 'Cockadoodle doo' – my signature tune.

But you know what betrayal is like? Did you ever stop suddenly in a shop or round the kitchen and redden again at the thought of something you did?

I'll never forget how he looked at me. I never boasted again.

I thought it might have changed things between us – but it didn't. He seemed to trust me more afterwards – to be surer of me when I was less sure of myself. Maybe because I was less sure.

The only thing I was surer of after was his love – there's no other word for it. Because now I knew he knew the kind of me, and still loved me.

You know, you're actually easier when someone knows all of you and all about you, good and bad, the real you without any pretences – when there's nothing hidden and no hiding, like a perfect marriage I suppose. And you're absolutely sure that you're loved just because you're you and just you. And you're sure. So I suppose the crowing of the cock still knocks a start out of me but that's only the first thought. On second thoughts I smile.

Lord, Peter wasn't the only one who let you down. If you suffered pain for betrayal some of us had a bigger hand in it than Peter. There are things that you know I did and I know – but he doesn't know, she doesn't know, they don't know. Oh God I'd be ashamed if … but help me, forgive me. I'm not the best or the strongest. But remember Peter. There are a lot of us … we mean well.

My name is Pilate
Of course I remember the incident – can't forget it. Oh, they were out to get him all right. Interesting man – from Nazareth as I remember. Quite calm; liked him, sharp, strange. Then herself – the wife – with that dream. Funny that, frightened me a little.

The funny thing is – it's always the small things you remember – it suddenly struck me how much the Jews loved symbols. They really weren't listening to what I was saying, so I sent for water and washed my hands of the whole affair, a sacrament of non-responsibility. What? You say of irresponsibility? Oh, it's easy to say. 'Jesting Pilate,' someone said about me. Not true. It was no joke, let me tell you.

Afraid? Well if you want the truth – whatever that is – if you want the truth, yes, I was afraid.

Well I'm not the first or the last who succumbed to pressure. I had a lot of ancestors and even more descendants. Maybe we're related, you and I, closer than you'd care to admit, blood brother, sister under the skin.

Yes, condemn me again. People have always condemned me – it's a Christian tradition. Except him. He didn't. He just said 'if you only knew'.

> Lord, you know how easily we blame Pilate and act like him. I've given in when there was a lot less pressure on me: in big ways for money or power; in small ways – nice to the doctor's wife and not noticing the poor relation. Sorry about the truth, Lord, it got lost along the way sometimes. Your heart fell every time. You had hopes for me and I dashed them. I know you saw me when you saw Pilate. I've washed my hands too but they're not clean. (Lord, wash away my iniquity, cleanse me from my sin.) Oh Pilate, Oh brother.

I am one of the thieves
No, I'm not Dismas – not the good guy. Nobody knows my name. Just as well. They wouldn't thank me where I come from. I caused them enough trouble without getting my name in the news. Anyway, it'd look funny, me with my name in the gospel – the good news. I'm bad news. The failure, the thief; the double failure, the thief that was caught – nails in me hands and a chip on me shoulder

and dying in company that's not of my choosing. Jesus – Christ – King: that's a laugh. But I'm not laughing.

There's no justice. What did I do? No chance ever. The father – sure he'd kill me if he got me. And the mother – maybe if she'd lived it'd have been different. Maybe it'd have been home at home – like, a nice place, like you'd imagine inside the curtains in a lighted room with people laughing and happy, and plenty to eat and warm as toast, and shoes on your feet that would keep the wet out, that keeps the nails out …

Dreams. Ah shut up, shut up, Dismas. Paradise! What are you trying to do? Steal your way to heaven?

C'mon Christ, save us so! Get off the Cross – and save us! Save us! See. No answer. No come down. No chance. No hope. No paradise.

> But if only there were. Oh God, if only … Lord, remember us who can't pray to you and who can do nothing but doubt you. Remember us who can do nothing but curse the Cross. Your laws seem too strong, wrong for us – we can't keep them. We're the faithless, the hopeless, the loveless. We're outside the door in the dark, at the edge of the crowd. Remember us, Lord. Remember! Maybe that's too strong – only don't forget us – we're yours too. We can't live in your company – maybe we can some day die in it.

My name is Judas
Well yes, it's a dirty word. I blame myself completely of course. Hanging here between heaven and earth gives you a different view of reality.

I did like the money, I admit it freely. Nothing wrong with that. Somebody has to look after it. Bursar, housekeeper, home economist, treasurer, banker, minister for finance – all necessary and respectable names.

But it grows on you. Money, I mean. You get some, you want more, and you don't like to see your stock of it dwindling. It takes on a life of its own.

But it wasn't the money. Thirty pieces of silver – well, I threw it back at them, didn't I?

They were going to get him anyway. I simply took advantage of the inevitable, to make a little on the side. It was easy money, money for old rope, as you say. As it turned out I didn't need it for the rope. They gave me enough rope and I – well, you know my story.

Lonely at the end. No one wanted me. But that wasn't the bad part. It was the blood on my hands. I sent him to die and he had done me, done nobody, wrong. And I couldn't undo it. I couldn't face back. I couldn't go back. There was no going back. I gave the kiss of death. I chose the dark.

> Lord, Judas was only the first. We have all betrayed love – made false promises, given lies for truth, broken hearts by treachery. Your pain is the strength of all that say 'I love you' and tell the truth; your pain is the forgiveness of all our failures. Remember again with pity those of us who have blood on our hands, who have betrayed love or destroyed innocence, or murdered friendship. And pity above all those who think there is no way back, those who have stepped into the dark, and who despair. Throw them a new rope, Lord. Draw them to you again and give them the kiss of life.

Good Friday

We were there when they crucified you, Lord. Bits of us in all the groups at the foot of the Cross. The small group, his friends, closest to the Cross. Would you be comfortable there?

Or would you be more comfortable in a bigger group, with those who wanted him out of the way, those he made uncomfortable. They shout and threaten but you don't have to. You can be civilised about it, if you like. Ignore him. Finally he'll die away. (Only thing is, he can rise again – in a pain, in a child, in a love, in a danger, in some desperate need, in a First Communion, in a death.)

Or you could join the army – the Roman army. 'I'm a soldier. Don't like these crucifixions. Take too long. We're here since twelve o'clock and its nearly three now. But the weekend's free. Deal out the cards again. We'll deal you in if you like.'

Sometimes I'm with the soldiers. Not much interested in you, Christ – you're a job, a chore. 'There are Stations at three o'clock' – 'Oh, why bring that up? We're going to Dublin for the weekend.' It's a long, long way from Calvary to here.

Sometimes I'm with the biggest crowd of all. Onlookers, watching, silent, puzzled, not for or against or callous, but needing you.

Needing your peace in my heart, needing your presence in my home, needing your grace in my life, needing your mercy for my sins, needing your pity for my weakness, needing your courage to carry on, needing your help for those I love, needing your patience, needing your kindness, needing your love. We too fall on the way. We need a hand, Lord. From your Calvary stretch your hand to ours.

We adore thee, O Christ, and we bless thee. Because by thy holy Cross thou hast redeemed the world.

Every Bush Burns

Vol. 45, No. 1, January 1994

How are you? Ah, don't answer me. It would mean nothing if you all answered together, and if you told me individually we'd be here a long time – we'd need a novena of our own. Anyway, you didn't come here to tell me how you are – you came to tell Mary, the Mother of God, and you don't have to wait your turn with her. Like mothers everywhere she can listen to and notice all her children at the same time and, what's more, when you tell her how you are, she's not just interested, she can always *do* something about it as well. She can turn to her Son and say, 'Look, they have no wine.' Through her the wine flowed at Cana, and it flows at Knock.

So how are you? No, don't answer me. But if you were to answer I'd say nearly all the Irish people here would say things like 'Not bad', or 'Oh, middling', or 'Fair', or that very detailed description 'Fair to middling.' Oh, there'd be maybe an odd American who'd say 'Fine', and an odd English person who'd say 'Marvellous'. But not the Irish. No, we might have a few who'd say, 'OK' – but no higher than that. We're very careful people. We don't give high marks easily and we don't like to tempt fate to upset our apple cart. There's an Irish feeling that if you're lucky enough to have an apple cart, keep quiet about it. We're strong believers that pride comes before a fall. Someone said the Irish suffer from bad memories. Not that we forget, not that we don't remember, but that we have long memories for bad things that happened to us. We pay more attention to Good Friday than to Easter Sunday.

A woman who came from Continental Europe to live in a small Irish town told me how welcome her neighbours made her; they were very nice to her. One of them brought her to tea and had all her friends in to meet her. And they talked after, and the talk turned to what was the most important moment in life and the Irish women agreed it was the moment after death, the moment when you met God in judgement, the particular judgement. That, for these Irish women, was the most important moment in life: the moment after death. We're wary of God. The young woman told me she wasn't sure she believed in the same God as the women. She said she believed in a God who loved her and they seemed to believe in a God you had to be afraid of, a bit anyway.

So how are you? Do you believe in this God that Moses spoke with? Moses said to God, 'Who will you send with us on the journey?' and God said, 'I will go with you myself' and went as a cloud by day and a pillar of fire by night. Is this the God we believe in, an accompanying God travelling with us night and day, with us all the way? Or have we allowed the darkness of life to hide the true God, and has fear replaced faith, and has the good news Christ brought gone stale – yesterday's newspaper and no good news on today's? Seeing the grief and missing the glory? And yet St Paul cries out, 'Glory to him whose power working in us can do infinitely more than we can ask or imagine.' Or imagine. Do we ever imagine God smiling?

Sometimes our souls grow small and our imaginations fail. There's more to our God than meets the eye, and we can suffer from the blindness of those who see only the visible. Our eyes always need opening. For the God to whom Moses said, 'Remember these are your people', that God accompanies his people still, and that God accompanied his people on a journey to a new land, to a new life, not on a journey to death. God does no less for us. He is a God of the living, not a God of the dead.

The cloud and the fire have gone. God travels with us now in the sacraments. With water, with oil, with bread, with word – and always for life.

And Christ is the God we meet in the sacraments, in these seven signs – those seven symbols of Incarnation, of God with us. For the sacraments are seven Christmases, seven Canas, seven Calvaries, seven Easters – seven signs of God's presence like Christmas; God's care, like Cana; God's love, like Calvary; and God's life, like Easter. Rightly we say we *celebrate* the sacraments – we have the right word, the word for being delighted that God is with us.

God With Us: the Christmas name for Christ. The angels celebrated it, we celebrate it: God's coming in to our human family, taking on the beauty and the burden of human flesh. The Word was made flesh and came to live among us. God and we were family again at last. Now the sacraments are the continuation of God's presence, and the fulfilment of Christ's promise, 'I am with you always.'

The sacraments are the familiarity of God with his people. God is family, not by marriage but by blood. Christ didn't make us in-laws. He made us sons, daughters, brothers, sisters. God is family and the sacraments are the commerce of love – the marking of milestones and the blessing of the humdrum; wedding cake one day, home-made bread the next, there's a sacrament for each. God has the recipe for both.

Sometimes I think we imprison God in seriousness. Heaven is not dull and the truth is that God, like us, enjoys baptism, confirmations, weddings.

Baptism is God delighted with the baby, welcoming the baby into his own family, asking 'Who have we here? What are ye calling him?' God saying, 'Do you know who he looks like? He looks like myself, he's the image of me.' God is part of the joy, the hope, the love that surrounds this new creation – joining the chorus of care that cossets this new life and saying again, 'This is good.'

Confirmation, and God delights in a grown body, product of twelve years of care and cut knees and kisses to make all wounds better. And here she is, she in the suit and the higher heels and the touch of lipstick, the suggestion of eyeshadow, and God saying, taking the words out of her parents' mouths, 'Look at her now, isn't she something? We'll have to mind her, get a cross dog; and may she be wise and understanding and good.' God looking at his girl and saying 'That is good.' That's Confirmation.

And the sacraments are personal – never God saying, 'You down there!' Never God saying, 'I'll never forget what's-his-name.' No, God doesn't forget, and he knows the name. It isn't just that Christ has us on the tips of his fingers. We're carved on the palms of his hands. Baptism itself is the very contradiction of anonymity – we are baptised by name, and confirmed by name, anointed by name, ordained by name, and nobody gets married by saying, 'I – *don't mind my name* – take you – *whatever your name is* – as my ...' Marriage is not for unknown quantities. And in Communion and penance, it is you who receives, it is you who gets absolution;

they're between God and you. Someone said, 'Not to be noticed is death.' The sacraments are God noticing: the sacraments are for life.

An American government official once asked Mother Teresa, 'How do you expect to feed these thousands of starving people?' and Mother Teresa answered, 'One by one.' That's God's way with us, one by one, except of course when we want to be two by two.

A wedding, and a new life for two people and God part of it – God saying what the fathers and mothers are saying, 'I hope they'll be happy, and they're going to need all the help they can get.' And God blesses them, 'This is my beloved son, my beloved daughter, in whom I am well pleased.'

And well-pleased is God to travel with them on their journey. 'Who will you send with them?' said Moses, and God said, 'I will go myself.' He will be there in the everyday like the bread, as the bread, part of their communion. He will be there as forgiveness to repair the wear and tear of life. He will be there as healer, in sickness coming with oil and word and touch. Our God stays in touch. For he is promised to them for life as they are promised to each other, and he makes the promise to them that they make to each other – to be with them in sickness and in health, for better, for worse, richer or poorer until they reach at last not death but new life.

The sacraments are not just monuments to a moment. They are for life and living. But not just because they do things for us or to us; they're more than that – they are God's headlines for us. You remember the old headline copies that taught us to write. You copied the beautifully written headline: 'All that glistens is not gold', 'He who hesitates is lost'; copied it with pen held grimly and your tongue sticking out the side of your mouth with the effort. The sacraments are God's headlines, and we live as images of God when we copy his headlines.

Baptism is the sacrament of welcome, and every time we welcome, every time we greet someone with word or smile, we take a leaf out of God's book and give new life. We are meant to be not just baptised people, but baptising people. We baptise at home, in shops, on the street – when we notice, accept, welcome, greet – and everyone is the better for it, baptiser and baptised. Oh it's good, as God would say, and you know the feeling yourself.

And we confirm: oh, you don't need to be a bishop, or a priest in an emergency. You'll meet people in need of confirmation every day, needing the word to encourage, needing the praise that raises the heart, the spirit – people needing the charism of your affirmation in a thousand ways. And you know yourself the life it gives, like the Holy Spirit. 'How are you? Oh, you look great. I love that blouse on you. Where did you get the suit? And how are you?' You're confirmed – you know the feeling. And perhaps you know the opposite, the death of 'Oh, what did you do to your hair?' There's a story of the little boy who got a present of a bow and arrow, and wanted his father to come out to play with it. His father was reading the paper and said, 'Ah, go out yourself. Anyway only one's needed to play with a bow and arrow.' And the little boy said, 'No, you need two – me to shoot and you to say "Great shot".' What sacrament did the little boy need? Confirmation, and God thinks it very good when we confirm one another and make every day a new Pentecost and bring the Holy Spirit down, you might say, at the drop of a hat. 'Oh, that hat looks lovely on you.' A compliment can be the grace of God.

And you know the resurrection that forgiveness brings when you long for someone's absolution – you break the Waterford glass vase, you scrape the pillar with the car, or is it scrape the car with the pillar? You didn't get the 'C' grade you hoped for, and someone who matters to you says, 'Arrah, what about it, it'd be worse if you broke your leg; isn't it great that you're all right? I'd rather have you than a million 'C's – that's absolution like God's absolution with love, and like God's it takes away guilt and gives new life.

Oh, and we have the anointing of one another too – in our hands, our words, our eyes, our faces. The grace of God can flow through us, for we can be living sacraments, sacramentalising all the moments of our day, bringing, being the power of God to redeem our time.

Like Christ, you say 'This is my body' to create a communion with a handshake or a hug. You do it getting the dinner for them, you do it putting up a shelf for her, bringing in the turf, tying a child's shoelace – this is my body, giving, given up for someone. This is gift, like Christ's gift, for the sake of someone else. This is my body, this is me, here I am, Lord, I have come to do your will – hot in the kitchen, cold in the field, bent over a desk, or a bed, or a stick. This is the everyday Eucharist and it has millions of celebrants, and God gives thanks for every one of them – the

Eucharist of heaven celebrating the Eucharists of earth. These are the sacraments of the continuous present. This is the imitation of Christ.

So, how are you? Maybe I should put the question another way. What have you to celebrate? In an old Greek play there is a woman who has lost everything – and the chorus say to her, 'What is left? Everything is destroyed, everything is gone.' She faces them and says, 'What is left? There is me.'

The sign of the Cross is the sign under which we are all born – and no doubt it is often the dominant sign in the lives we live. We each have our own cross, shaped and made to measure. So what have you to celebrate? What's left? There's you – and you God celebrates, celebrates you with sacraments, travelling with you from beginning of life here to end of life here, seeing you safely to the beginning of new life, for our imitation of Christ doesn't stop at the grave. There's you – you friend of God, travelling through life with God. 'Who will you send with us?' said Moses. 'I'll go myself,' said God. There's you, you empowered by God, to be sacrament to the world.

So how are you? You to whom God has given the power through his Spirit for your hidden self to grow strong. How are you? You in whose heart Christ lives, you who are filled with the utter fullness of God. Are you really only fair, only middling, only fair to middling?

I think the right answer, the real answer, is another Irish answer, the one in which grace breaks through our Celtic darkness. How are you? Great, thank God, great.

Hearing Confessions

Vol. 45, No. 5, May 1994

O Lord, open my lips. This is only a starter – a sort of *hors d'oeuvres varthe* – different things to reflect on in our hearing of confessions. I won't be talking about everything and I won't be putting things in order of importance. It's only a starter – not the main course (soul on the bone? Or perhaps mixed grille?) – but still, I hope, food for thought.

First let me confess – that I claim no special expertise or charism in the matter of hearing confessions. I have heard more confessions than some of you, and far fewer than many of you. And I hear confessions in my way, and you in yours, and none of us maybe is a man for all penitents but there is still common ground and in that ground I hope something I say may confirm you in your practice and experience – where you'll say to yourself, 'That's the way it is for me too' and be glad to know it is. I hope as well that my way of hearing or my way of thinking about hearing will throw a sidelight on yours, and that later you may do as much for me, help me to freshen my words, or deepen my understanding or increase my compassion.

But for the moment this is my confession. I hope to make it honestly, and that may mean foolishly because, as you know, we say things inside in confession that could sound very stupid outside – so I'm looking for absolution too, and in advance. I won't be developing anything at length, and I thought that what I'd do would be to give a sort of slide show. It seemed an appropriate image – though it is no longer part of Knock confessionals – because the slide in the confessional was like the old slide projector. You pushed the slide and a totally new image appeared, you pushed again and it was another image. And the slide in the confessional was like that – go in peace – the closing for one story, one life, shutter shut; shutter open, and other story, another life. Bless me father. How long since ...?

Slide one: God at Work

There is no other place in a priest's life where God is so obviously present. I'm talking first of all of those moments every priest knows when, to his wonder, he has spoken with words that have been given him to speak, and moments when he knows God has touched and changed a human life, years and weight of guilt dissolving into joy. We have all been touched and elated by these moments. We have come back like the seventy-two, we can report people cured, and demons subject to us in Christ's name, and Christ sees Satan fall like lightning from heaven again.

But God is present in every confession. It's his place of course, but sometimes you can get so used to someone's being there that you only miss them when they're gone. It's worth thinking of the enormous grace at work in the most ordinary of confessions – the one you've heard a thousand times, and maybe made a few times too. It is extraordinary that someone you've never met, or someone you know and who knows you know them, will walk in, cold, and tell you as truly as they can most intimate details, catalogue their meanness, drag their dark into the light, share secrets not even their closest relations or friends know – that is extraordinary. It is amazing that after a ritual, perfunctory 'Bless me Father for I have sinned', things are told that the wildest horses would not drag out. That's God at work – the immediate creation of trust, the power of God establishing a road on which his grace may run. People say to us sometimes, as a joke, 'Ye have the power.' As you know it is a joke and we haven't much. But there we do, in the confessional – and it's not ours, and it is ours. It's the same power that excited the seventy-two and that Christ came through closed doors to give his disciples. Through closed doors. There's a thought. God at work. Next slide, please.

Slide two: Confessors I have known

It's worth considering what sort of confessor pleased yourself or displeased yourself. It's a good mirror into which to look – and to walk away remembering, not forgetting.

We've all heard horrific stories of confessors who reduce people to tears or worse. We know that no sacrament was ever meant to reduce anyone. A few years ago I asked a number of people to write about confessors – I wanted their views for a talk I was giving. I looked at what they wrote again last night. They were almost all very complimentary – talking of help and understanding and sympathy and kindness. That made the exceptions stand out even more starkly. A couple of phrases: 'he gave off to me', 'this priest attacked me', 'he was a kind of ecclesiastical Jaws'. Not quite the ideal experienced in the Letter to the Hebrews – one who is able to deal patiently with erring sinners for he himself is beset by weakness.

I have had only a couple of experiences of feeling 'attacked' myself. One was oddly enough in St Peter's in Rome a few years ago. It can happen anywhere. I didn't think I had told the confessor anything extraordinary, certainly nothing different from what I had told to assorted Carmelites and Augustinians and Jesuits and Redemptorists over the years. They hadn't batted an eyelid at what I told them – at least I didn't hear it batting. But this priest in Rome batted me. He berated me for my failures, and it surprised me because I wasn't accustomed to it and I didn't think they were really wicked. I didn't much mind it and the sharp shock of a kind of reality therapy was perhaps salutary too. But this priest also said something which I question while he was giving off to me. He said, 'Of course we know the mercy of God is infinite, but how do we know it extends to you?' I had a vision as I listened to him of God's mercy as either infinitely long and narrow, or infinitely wide and short – and me in no-mercy land. I question his vision of God's mercy but it all made me think how important to our hearing of confessions is our own vision of God. What God do we represent in confession? What's our vision of God? It will make a difference. Check vision.

Lately I went to confessions in Ireland. I met a no-nonsense confessor – a sort of 'give me the facts' man. He thundered at me. I prefer the voice of God in the gentle wind but, of course, God has spoken in thunder too – and this time anyway he was not saying 'This is my beloved son in whom I am well pleased.'

Maybe again the experience was salutary – at least because it made me aware again of the sort of confessor I did not want to be and maybe – you can have your own opinion – of the sort of confessor that should not be. I think that finally the sacrament of penance is a sacrament of the love of God, and that ultimately the confessor representing that God, must, should in some way love the penitent.

I'll mention briefly a few other confessors I have known. There was a confessor I remember from a retreat long ago who in his niceness refused to let me own my guilt. I felt guilty – over what I have forgotten – and in some way he refused to hear my confession of it, and I came out only with my penance, making 'satisfaction' but dissatisfied. And then there were all the yawning confessors – the ones who came out to hear you in the parlour of some religious house and that you felt you had interrupted, taken away from their spiritual reading or whatever. There were among them the perfunctory, the casual, the uninterested – God bless you, off you go and let me back.

There are bits of all these and other bits too in me at times. It will happen to us all at times. We are not always at our best. But it's good to look in the mirror and not forget. Next slide please.

Slide three: The good confessor
The confessor is the penitent's expectation of Christ. The good confessor is the one who lives up to that expectation – patient, compassionate, merciful teacher, guide, encourager. Fill it out of your own vision. Fr John Shea says somewhere that Christ was a man people came to with their burdens: the troubled in body, soul and mind, the disappointed, the upset parents, wives with husbands who wouldn't talk, husbands with wives who wouldn't stop, came to talk about stock that was lost, and land that wouldn't grow wheat, and fig trees that failed, and wine that was short, and lives that were gone crazy. He was a man people came to and he heard them all and he didn't shout at them and they were glad they came. A good confessor, Christ. Next slide please.

Slide four: The penitent. Who's that there?
This is a human being affected by Calvary. This is someone sent here by God. This is someone who at this moment is where God wants him to be. This is someone who is sorry for sin, and who wants to be free of it. This is someone who wants, feebly or desperately or

somewhere in between, to be a new creation. So this is someone whose life at this moment is a meeting place for God's hopes and desires and human hopes and desires. Pope John Paul, I think, said of penance that it was an exercise of a gift given by God, a human being's right to a more personal encounter with the crucified, forgiving Christ. And here he is. Make him welcome. Next slide please.

Slide five: The penitent talking
Often you could tell it for them, for you have heard it or them a thousand times before. You could tell it for them too because it's your own story, and Adam's and Eve's. But similarity or predictability does not take away individuality. This man's story, this woman's story, is their unique individual gift to God – an offering of the self, the truest self, 'this is me'. An offering never to be rejected, always respected.

What or who are they looking for? 'Who' is easy in one way. They're looking for Christ in some guise. But what guise? Well, I think not exactly a mechanic for repair, not just a judge for decision and not only a physician for healing either. I think they're looking for someone who can raise them from the dead. Penance is the resurrection sacrament.

Resurrection? Somebody put words into Martha's mouth. 'Resurrection! A neat idea,' Martha said, 'but will it work with someone this dead?' Jesus spoke and Lazarus came out bound in bands of stuff and Jesus said, 'Untie him, let him go free.' The confessor is to be someone who speaks Jesus' words again, someone who is an agent of resurrection.

Resurrection? People look to Christ for a new beginning, a fresh start, the grace of encouragement, and the encouragement of grace. 'A second baptism', the Fathers called penance – freedom and new life again. So penance is to restore possibility to the future, to take the past out of the present, and make it past forever. And all this in five minutes? Who do they think we are? Who do we think we are? Well, we're not on our own. Next slide please.

Slide six: The Confessor talking – and listening
And the Word became flesh. A famous Jewish Rabbi said, 'God's gift of the power of speech was as important as the creation of the word.' Indeed, the early Aramaic translation of the Genesis phrase that Adam became 'a living being' reads 'Adam was given the spirit of speech.' And we begin the Office or the Rosary as the Jews begin their worship with 'O Lord, open my lips.'

The confessor's words are to carry the compassion of Christ. Someone defined compassion as 'where hurt links arms with love'. We're very close to the Letter to the Hebrews again – dealing patiently with erring sinners because he himself is beset by weakness. Another book of the Hebrews, the Talmud, says that each year the High Priest, before he was to enter the Holy of Holies to pray for the people, would spend the evening with the elders of Israel. They would remind him of the responsibilities he bore and the elders would cry with him. If he could not weep he was not worthy.

An old story, but I think it has something to say to a confessor, who is trading in old stories. He must listen and then speak with a catch in his throat. The oldest story has a penitent's explanation, 'I was naked so I hid.' We must help people to come out of hiding. The right words are a help. 'O Lord, open my lips.' God told Moses to speak to the rock and it would bring forth water. Moses struck the rock – God would have preferred that he speak to it. The Word was God's way. The rod was Moses' way. We must never see the sacrament as a way of making people pay.

So sometimes in our speaking it is more compassionate not to pursue people. Not to ask can be more compassionate than to ask. And where asking must be done it should be a compassionate archaeology – careful. Sensitive, sifting, small trowel not bulldozer.

And listening. Not to be heard is death. So listening should be active, and that's so easy to say, and often so difficult to do. The brain can slip so easily into neutral, and the tongue speak 'a ready rhetoric, salve for all wounds'. Someone has said, 'In a world without God there is no one to hear.' Penance is the world with God, and in the confessional you are now God listening, speaking, 'hearing', as we say ourselves. O Lord, open my lips. Next slide please.

Slide seven: Me
There's another Jewish story of two Jews listening to a third who is praying and saying to God, 'God, I am a sinner. I am nothing.' And, one of the listeners turns to the other and says 'Will you look who thinks he's nothing?'

No confessor is nothing. But it is still true that I'm not going to succeed with everyone, be just the person this penitent needs. There are better than me. And I know there are times I asked the wrong question, the tone was wrong or I misjudged – anyway something was wrong and the blinds came down. I've met penitents I didn't know exactly what to say to or do for, and in that situation I can only ask, tritely or contritely but importantly: what would Christ do? He'd be compassionate anyway. Compassion never goes astray. Next slide please.

Slide eight: Me again
What does the penitent do for me? I think God never lets us approach each other with empty hands – he always gives us something to give, like a mother sending her child to a party. And every penitent re-ordains us. The faith and need of a confessing community ordain us again. 'You have been taken from among people and ordained for people in the things that are God's. Bless me Father for I have sinned.' Ionesco said, 'Everything is expressible in words – except the living truth.' I think you need someone, a person, for that, which is why God sent Christ, and why Christ sends people on all kinds of mission. And when all is said I think that's why Christ sends us into confessionals, so that we can be the living truth of God's forgiveness and mercy and love. O Lord, open my lips. And my tongue shall announce your praise.

An Accompanying God

Vol. 45, No. 10, October 1994

Survival or Salvation? A Second Mayo Book of Theology (Enda McDonagh, Columba Press, 1994) is a book to set the mind racing. It is not a sequel to the first book, a sort of *The Godfather: Part II* following the success and pattern of *The Godfather*. Rather it is a consequence. The first book was a book of courtiers gathered round theology, the Queen of Sciences, the ministers of the Queen, celebrating, meditating, considering, enlightening, delighting in. But in the second book the Queen leaves her throne, rolls up her sleeves, and moves from the throne to the kitchen, and theology, if it is to fulfil itself, must get into the kitchen because that's where God spends most of His/Her time, an equal opportunities Creator.

Not that there is a word about kitchens in the book. But a man who wrote a book recently about the old Greek myths quoted a remark in defence of their relevance: 'These things never happened but are always.' The things in *Survival or Salvation?* are a truth beyond that, for all in this book happened, is happening, and will happen always and everywhere.

President Mary Robinson, who is of Mayo, and who so memorably in her inauguration address said she was of Ireland and invited the world to dance with her in Ireland, wrote the foreword to this *Second Mayo Book of Theology*. In that foreword she admirably and precisely points out the cosmic and universal sense of all that is said in the book in different Mayo accents – 'the way in which the concerns of one part of the world are mobilised by imagination and expression to reach well beyond it'. She remarks later that the worldwide issue does not erase the parochial and the parochial does not block out the global. In other words if it is of Mayo, it is of Ireland and of the world. 'They are parts of one another,' she says, 'whose relation needs to be affirmed by imagination and compassion at all times, as it is here.'

I think all that needs to be said when describing this book, because one might think that a *Faith and the Hungry Grass: A Mayo*

Book of Theology was by Mayo people about Mayo people and Mayo concerns and of interest only to Mayo people. That would be untrue – as untrue as saying that the Bible is a Hebrew Book of Theology written largely by Hebrews for Hebrews about Hebrews and of interest only to Hebrews. The Bible is about God and God's people and this Mayo Book is, like the Bible, about God and God's people.

One of the old Christian Doctrine attributes of God was that God is omnipresent, which, in the way we learned it, stressed that God was everywhere as a presence, a sustaining presence but also a sort of minatory presence. You couldn't open your mouth but God heard you. God was everywhere, the unseen listener at every conversation. As we learned that, I think we missed the larger loving meaning of God's omnipresence: that God is with his people in everything, an accompanying God, who is never uninterested or disinterested but always part of every situation. I think this book brings that home to us, brings God home to us and us home to God. We are all in this together and God is not a tough judge but engaged with us in the struggle, engaged by Creation and Incarnation.

This Mayo book is like the Bible as it restores this truth to us. But even in its plan and concern and conclusion it will remind you of the Bible from beginning to end. Fancifully, the President in her foreword looks at the whole Mayo creation and finds it good, and the book ends with a consideration of *Apocalypse Now* by the editor. He finishes with a vision and a hope that 'Mayo people and their island-wide, worldwide winter companions may finally escape that long winter confinement, not only to survive but to flourish.' The dragons will be defeated, Mayo God help us, and 'Hope is the winter name of God.'

In between genesis and apocalypse, there are the old stories of the Bible. The stories of exile and exodus are here, the chronicles, stories of names and places and people, books of the kings and the queens, like Granuaile. There is the movement through the deserts of poverty and lack of education to visions of new lands and riches. There are the prophets! John Patrick Lyons, a liberation theologian in another century; Ethna Viney writes on holy mountains as is only right in any Bible; Pat Rabbitte like an Amos or Jeremiah looks to the regeneration of Mayo Israel; Andy Greeley writes the book of numbers; Nuala Bourke wants the search for the living God to be done by Moses with the people – with them, not wrestling with them or being wrestled by them; Pádraig Flynn is part of the wisdom literature, writing on the relevance of the local, not just a meditation on Tip O'Neill's 'All politics is local' but a searching out of the strength and meaning of the human being who stands firmly in faith and fatherland, a strength and meaning which drives away suspicion and fear of others, and allows understanding and acceptance, and awards one the freedom to be the image of the accepting God who is the God of all people, shepherd of all flocks, not just the one your dog pens.

Finally, there is the book of Ruth, indeed a few books of Ruth. Ruth said to Naomi: 'Your people shall be my people.' So the two of them went on until they came to Bethlehem, a place – Chesterton said – where all men are at home ('The House of Christmas', G. K. Chesterton). President Robinson in her foreword remarks on Mayo at work in Africa, in China, in Latin America. There is a phrase I grew up with, maybe a Mayo phrase, or an Irish phrase, or one used the world over, a phrase of Christ-compassion: 'My heart went out to him / her / them.' This Mayo book is full of the heart going out, going out to past and future in pity, in pride and in hope, going out to the underprivileged and the unfairly treated, to the suffering and the separated and very notably to specific communities and people as Ruth's heart went out to Naomi. Suzanne Ryder's heart goes out to Peru, John Blowick's heart went out to China sixty years earlier, Máiréad McDonagh's goes out to Somalia and Ethiopia. Perhaps Máiréad's story of giving her blood to save the life of a Muslim woman named Fatima whose grieving husband was a man named Mahomet, in its fact and in its symbolism with all the resonances of the deed and the names, sums up that Mayo of the spirit whose heart goes out to all the world and makes it one, at odd moments anyway, a glimpse of the hope of Christ, a glimpse of the hope of the world.

Not all the articles in the book will appeal to everyone. Mayo people will naturally find themselves more immediately at home with some of them. Someone whose interest is history or sociology, somebody who is from Chicago or Killasser will find particular articles of particular interest. The great triumph of the book, however, is that it outs God on the front page, and all the other pages. God is not confined to a column by our Religious Affairs correspondent but part of all the life he created and in which he is so often unnoticed, and his presence unbelieved and unbelievable. The editor is to be congratulated on finding and showing us so many burning bushes. While books like this can be written I think its title could well be not 'Survival or Salvation' but 'Survival *and* Salvation', because this book is evidence of both.

Christmas: What's Yours?

Vol. 45, No. 12, December 1994

There are a lot of Christmases. There's the quiet one, which occurs for most people every year and yet always seems to be spoken of as if it came as a surprise: 'Wasn't it a very quiet Christmas this year?' 'Oh indeed, sure it's over before you know it, after all the preparation.' There's the child's Christmas – not quiet at all, a Christmas of glistening eyes, and lit faces, and hopes, and excitement that turns to tiredness and crying, and overeating that satiates or sickens children of all ages. There's the drinking Christmas too, excuse for some, tiring round for others, 'habitually cited as exhausting and rarely as satisfying', as an American writer says (Anna Quindlen, 'There Isn't Any Room at the Inn', *Gainsville Sun*, 22 December 1991).

There's the homecoming Christmas too which touches in its way – I mean its unconscious, unaware way – the Christmas that God began. It's a Christmas orchestrated by those who prepare and wait for and welcome in their own particular Bethlehem and by those who prepare and travel gift-bearing *to* their own particular Bethlehem, expecting, hoping for welcome and for love to bathe them in its care and delight and the comfort of being home at last.

'Gather the people, break the bread, tell the story' was, I understand, an old summary of the Mass. One way or another the world celebrates at least the second syllable of Christmas, and I don't think you can really separate the syllables completely. I think Christ gets in to our Christmas willy-nilly. Oh, there are terrible Christmases in some homes. Christmas and Calvary, but in the world as a whole Christ achieves some sign of his promise to the world, in the gathering, in the breaking of bread together, in the story written by someone's love for someone.

Then there's the real Christmas, the one that began with the first one and still happens every year. God comes as Christ to join the human race. From Pope John Paul's telling one would believe that it was a difficult coming for God and remains so. Oh, he made it look simple and that's the way we see it – the world coos over babies. But we don't spend our lives cooing and babies hear harsher sounds very soon. God, the Pope suggests, did not find it easy to insinuate himself into the human race. He had to keep working at it and it took him thirty-three years. Christmas was only fully achieved on Calvary when Christ had failed enough and died enough to be fully one of us. 'In a certain sense,' says the Pope, 'God has gone too far!' becoming a stumbling block to the Jews and foolishness to the Gentiles.

We don't like to let people get too close to us; closeness means not just invasion of our space, and so loss of a freedom, but it means challenge and obligation too. Christ, says the Pope, elicits the impression that it was too much … 'Man was no longer able to tolerate such closeness.'

'And thus,' says Pope John Paul, 'the protests began … This great protest has precise names – first it is called the Synagogue and then Islam. Neither can accept a God who is so human. "It is not suitable to speak of God in this way" they protest, "he must remain absolutely transcendent, he must remain pure majesty. Majesty, full of mercy, certainly, but not to the point of paying for the faults of his own creatures, for their sins."' (*Crossing the Threshold of Hope*, p. 41)

There are lesser protests. Ours is the Christian one. It's not the transcendence of God that worries us but the transparency of God, making it so clear to us what Christmas really is and should be each year and always. So let's look at our Christmas. What's Christmas anyway?

As this world goes, Christmas – the first Christmas and still the real Christmas – is the feast of the inappropriate and the unexpected. As this world thinks, you wouldn't expect God to be born in a stable, or to live a friend of sinners, or to die among thieves. As far as this world goes, you mightn't expect God at all, but God came – in the flesh. That's Christmas for you – inappropriate, unexpected God turning up in an unexpected way, in an unexpected shape, in an unexpected place – that's Christmas for you, real Christmas, God with us.

Neither a borrower nor a lender be – this world's wisdom. But Christ comes, the Lord of the borrowed, a borrowed birthplace, a borrowed death-place too – manger, tomb. And he comes lending, lending grace and meaning to poverty, and all that goes with it, and all it goes without. Like all babies this baby tends to stand the world on its head, to ask for unreasonable sacrifice, to give unreasonable delight, unreasonable except that love, real love, goes way beyond reason. That's Christmas for you.

And did you notice what happens in this inappropriate place, with this unreasonable child: reconciliations take place that reason could never achieve – it takes love. In the stable even the animals lie unhunted, at peace with the human race. In the stable there's no competition between the man and the woman, only delight in the presence of a baby. In the stable there's no class war or class distinction and no division between home and away or between town and gown, there's place for shepherds from near and there's place for wise men from far and it's the same place. Kneeling by the baby they are at peace. That's Christmas for you.

It's that kind of place, this stable – a place that makes friends of all who gather there; a place of no jealousy; a place of the oldest story of human joy, oh! as old as Eden; a place of hope; a place of love; and a place of faith.

That's Christmas for you.

The unexpected God comes there, knowing no language but touch and look and sound. Would you ever expect a God who answers only to softness of skin, to gentleness of touch, to sweetness of look, inappropriate God? Their opposites, roughness, violence, anger, hate, have no power with this God – only the weak things of the world have power in this stable.

That's Christmas for you, God saying, 'Let's stay in touch.' That's what every baby cries for, babies of all ages, and God cries for it too. Christmas is the feast of staying in touch: heaven in touch with earth; God in touch with people; me in touch with you. By hand – sign of peace; by card – Christmas card; by phone – voices in the air, 'peace on earth'; by visit – the second joyful mystery; by gift – a star lighting darkness.

Mary's hand, Joseph's hand holding him, wrapping him, rocking him, cuddling him. Not God in an idea, but God in a word, God in a touch. 'Let's stay in touch' said God – for this is the closeness that consoles the crying, comforts the lonely and gives peace to the dying. That's Christmas for you.

But it needs someone, always someone, for softness of skin, for gentleness of touch, for sweetness of look, for kindness of voice. It needs someone, always someone, for reconciliation, and the healing of wounds and the making up of rows and the giving of peace. It needs someone, always someone, to light the road, to renew hope, to restore faith, to return love.

Christ came that first Christmas. It needs someone this Christmas too.

Thoughts on Sunday

Vol. 14, No. 2, February 1963

Fourth Sunday after Epiphany

We live in a world that, at its calmest, is on the edge of fear. Almost seasonally now it slips over the edge into crisis and panic. It's all rather like a scene from an old Western. The desperados eye each other warily, hand at holster, from opposite ends of the saloon. Play stops at the tables. The bartender, anxious, continues to polish a perfunctory glass and gets ready to duck under the counter. Except that the counter is no longer a safeguard, for now that the antagonists face each other across the world destruction may be instant and global and so men need deeper and deeper shelters for security.

And as the forces of destruction increase, the individual feels himself diminished. It isn't just the same diminution that men have always felt in the presence of the elemental, before the mass of a mountain, before the might of the sea. The smallness had in it no fear, only a calm in the presence of a greatness that savoured the unseen presence and the limitless greatness of God. But in the present diminution there is fear, occasional panic and the impotence of despair. God seems absent and there are moments when there is naught for our comfort,

> Save that the sky grows darker yet
> And the sea rises higher.

We are at such moments rather like the men in today's gospel – at the mercy of a storm, powerless before wind and wave, the frightened company of a sleeping God. It was for them a moment of terror, of quite literally mortal dread, and God lies asleep. Fishermen they were and knew the sea and knew their boat, and if they were in panic it was because every nerve and every sinew, every past minute of days and nights on this very sea, screamed at them that death clawed at their boat. And out of their collective panic and powerlessness breaks the shivering cry 'Lord, save us, we perish' – the *oratio recta* (direct speech) of the *De Profundis*.

And one man wakes Christ, and Christ says: 'Why are ye so fearful, O ye of little faith?' and with a word he calms the wind and sea. They would have rowed on then, in silence, a little ashamed as men always are after showing fear.

We know they had no reason to be afraid. We know that Christ asleep was no less protective and no less powerful than Christ awake. They were as safe with Christ in the storm as they were with Christ in the calm, for Christ is not merely man but also omnipotent God and is never unconcerned or oblivious.

It is a truth easily remembered and easily forgotten. The Christian parent forgets it sometimes in a sudden moment of fear for children in a world where evil seems to grow more powerful and alluring. It is forgotten sometimes by the priest in the moments of discouragement when he feels small and weak and alone before the rising tides of evil. Christianity looks at times and in moods almost a lost cause. Commandments seem so difficult to keep – how can the young survive? – isn't one only a small, at best grudgingly heeded voice in a roaring world?

That happens – but it is to forget that Christ is still with us, not merely a companion but a God, and might say again: 'Why are ye so fearful?' We suffer sometimes from the 'weakened belief' which Cardinal Suhard pinpointed, 'Our age has fortunately rediscovered the extraordinarily brotherly character of the Son of Man but misses the mystery of the Son of God.' We must remain aware that 'his immensity becomes the very motive of our security, our hope, our daring … It is his discreet and irresistible strength which works in us.'

Septuagesima Sunday
'That's not fair. He got more than me.' It's the child's complaint as the infant eye, with the deadly accuracy of self-interest, measures two pieces of cake or any given number of sweets. It's the child's complaint in the blatant, patent, obvious child's formula. The formula will change as the child grows up ('After all, I'm the one who …', 'Only for me he wouldn't be …') but the complaint will recur, for self-interest does not leave the normal eye and a keen sense of justice to one's ego remains with most of us to the end.

That's why perhaps we have a certain sympathy with the plaintiffs in today's gospel who 'thought that they should receive more … and murmured against the master of the house, saying: "These last have worked but one hour and thou hast made them equal to us who have borne the burden of the day and the heats."' In similar circumstances we might have felt like that ourselves. In similar circumstances perhaps we do feel like that. For humanity, with little to be jealous about, will be jealous about little, and so it is a work of human diplomacy to be careful of little differences in seniority and title and precedence.

By the mathematics of earth we can understand that those who worked the full day may feel slightly irked and cheated, for ours is a world of restrictive trade practices, 'closed shop' policies, 'time and a half'. The shop stewards might have had a word to say.

The lesson surely is that the mathematics of heaven and the gospel are different – the last shall be first, to him who hath much more shall be given, from him who hath little even that which he hath shall be taken away, you leave the ninety-nine and go after the one – the topsy-turvy scale which seems to set at naught the wisdom of earth, so that the wisdom of man is the folly of God. Hall and Knight could never have made a satisfactory problem out of this – A works eight hours and receives one penny, B works five hours and receives one penny, C works three hours and receives one penny, D works one hour and receives one penny – no problem, only a question: Why?

And the answer perhaps is a little light on the marvellous just-ice of God. Our little human justice can measure time and wages and work but not really a man's opportunity, a man's pain, a man's chance in life, not really the weight of one man's sorrow, the unique and individual tensions and stress of one man's mind. These are for us the imponderables. We do well to make allowances for them but our human Justitia carries no scale precise or delicate enough to do them justice. Only God can do that and God, as today's gospel tries to tell us, has a generosity and a justice which go beyond our petty human notions.

Like the vineyard owner he measures not only work done but the pain of waiting too, not only the employment but the pain of unemployment. The generosity of God is not circumscribed by human envies or jealousy. And it remains a chastening thought that Our Lord did say that the harlots would get into heaven before the scribes and Pharisees and that any suggestion of *seniores priores* (elders first) occurs only once in the gospel.

It is perhaps too a consoling gospel, one to set against that stark 'and every idle word that man shall speak he shall render an account ...' of the catechism – an answer that left one with a picture of a rather frightening schoolmaster going out of a classroom and warning: 'And if there's one word out of ye while I'm out ...'. But in today's gospel that picture is balanced. The good thoughts, the good wishes, the good words – account will be taken of these too.

Our justice, our order of things is so often a justice, an order, of mediocrity. We don't like people 'who step out of line'. People better than ourselves are often a reproach and a challenge we do not want to accept. Saints have always been the mavericks of society, disturbers of our peace. 'Is thine eye evil because I am good?' It's a danger for everyone, but perhaps especially for priests who have a professional interest in being good. We need a constant vigilance to ensure that our resistance to, our attacks on, the new ideas, the new movements, the extra efforts of others are not basically a defence of our own mediocrity, for as Father de Lubac remarks: 'Nothing is more ingenious, more obstinate, nastier – indeed, in a sense, more clear-sighted – than mediocrity harrying every form of superiority that offends it. There is nothing more demanding than the taste for mediocrity. Beneath its ever-moderate appearance there is nothing more intemperate; nothing surer in its instinct; nothing more pitiless in its refusals. It suffers no greatness, shows beauty no mercy.'

Sexagesima Sunday

I remember once talking to a priest about a book of sermons on the Sunday gospels which had just been published. He had looked it over and I asked him how he thought it would sell. He smiled and with the slight cynicism of experience said: 'Of course it will sell. Sermon books always sell well. There's as ready a market for tinned sermon as for tinned salmon – one for Friday, the other for Sunday.'

It was one of these by-no-means-fully-meant comments made for the pleasure of their tang rather than for their truth. Unfortunately or fortunately one never does find a ready-to-serve sermon. But most of us remember with gratitude, and maybe sometimes with a prayer, Msgr Knox, Fr Trese and the host of others who on a tired Saturday night (to tell the truth) have thrown us a thought to start a train and made what we did serve on Sunday morning a little more sustaining than it might otherwise have been.

Today's gospel of 'the sower who went out to sow his seed' must hold a special place in the affections of all those who publish sermons or sermon-notes – for it is their prototype and charter. The parable is that of the sower, with commentary and annotation by Christ himself. It is the moment when Christ touches the 'homily on the gospel' with a benediction and makes all of them part of his work forever.

This gospel has one other peculiar quality, its effect of a 'play within a play'! For, even as the preacher reads it and preaches on it he is re-enacting it. The reality accompanies the symbol. As soon as the priest faces his people from the pulpit or the altar-steps and says: 'The sower went out ...', then the sower goes out, sowing once again the word of God. In the faces before him the seed which is the word of God meets ground again – wayside, the rock, among thorns, good ground. They will all be there as Christ typed them two thousand years ago in Palestine – proudly in a furcoat, stiff under the guild banner, bending sideways to quieten a child, on one knee and a cap behind a pillar. But only God knows which is which.

And, lastly, there is this symbol of seed and growth which will recur again and again in Christian thought – the seed planted at baptism which is to flower in eternal life. The seed which is God's Word, the seed which is the body itself sown in corruption to rise in incorruption. Guitton quotes the inscription Claudel chose for his tombstone, 'Here lie the husk and the seeds of Paul Claudel' and remarks: 'What a fine definition of renewal! One part of the plant, the husk, decays; another part, the secret and seminal, the bud, breaks out' (*The Guitton Journals*, Jean Guitton, p. 308).

The congregation, the parish, is the seeding-ground of God. For the sower strewing seed it is an area rich in possibility, heavy with responsibility. In no other sermon of the year will he be so closely identified with Christ preaching – something to make him, as he faces his people, his particular piece of ground, at once proud and humble. Perhaps for the sower going up and down the conacre he has taken from God, the offertory which follows the gospel might be a personal: 'Perfect thou my goings in thy paths.'

Quinquagesima Sunday

Neither life nor literature much effects the happy ending and so there's an extra pleasure in today's true story of the cure of the blind man. No modern writer or film director would have finished a story or a scene like this with a cure. The scene, the behaviour of the crowd, the blind man shouting, demanding, being jostled, being rebuked – these they would have given us faithfully and artistically. But the blind man would have remained blind. The crowd would have moved on, leaving the helpless figure alone, and the terrible pleading voice would echo on in our memories and imaginations, to underline once again the hopeless hope of waiting for Godot or for anybody.

But the voice of today's blind man caught the ear of God. 'Nice guys finish last' is a modern sport proverb. This blind man was not 'a nice guy'. There is no meekness here, no gentle tapping of a white cane. This man wants one thing and he wants it badly. This man is one of the violent.

It is a noisy gospel, crowded with talk and people, but it is all dominated by one voice, a voice that is fierce, persistent, annoying. People try to stop him, and think of all the different ways a shoving crowd has of telling a man to keep quiet – and not one of them polite. This is a concerto for orchestra and soloist, but loud though the brass of those orchestra voices swell, still undrowned rises above them that cry from the soul of man: 'Jesus, Son of David, have pity on me.'

And then in a moment of magnificent silence Christ stands before the sightless eyes. God faces man, the Creator the created, light confronts darkness. 'What is it you want from me?' asks God. 'Lord,' says man, 'that I may see.'

When our minds quieten after the drama of that encounter, we may reflect once again on man's inhumanity to man and God's care even for those on the edge of the crowd. For the people who tried to prevent his cure, who rebuked him, who tried to keep his prayer from the ear of Christ, were his own people, the literal followers of Christ.

There is perhaps always the danger that the followers of Christ may be over-possessive of their truth and show scant courtesy to those on the edge of the crowd. In the modern wave of ecumenism and in the growth of greater Christianity among Christians the danger of that has perhaps lessened. Our ears have caught again some of Christ's acuteness of hearing and we have a greater sympathy and respect for him who wishes he could join with us in our following of Christ. But here in Ireland there is perhaps one person on the edge of the crowd of whom we have suspicion and to whom we sometimes show resentment – the lapsed or non-practising Irish Catholic. We sometimes feel in his case a sense of personal betrayal.

In our relations with other non-Catholic Christians – the 'lapsed Catholics' of four hundred or more years ago – 'dialogue has replaced diatribe', to quote Archbishop Heenan (*Liturgical Arts,* vol. 34, no. 2–4. p. 164). If with our own, recently 'lapsed Catholic' the dialogue is not possible, we should still at least not exclude him from the radius of our Christianity; at least we should in our own phrase 'bid him the hour of day'. For here too there is question of a man at the edge of the crowd, who was not meant to be rebuked by his own people, and we must be watchful not to interpose ourselves between Christ and a soul crying still, perhaps: 'Lord, that I may see.'

Homilies for Wedding Jubilees

Vol. 20, No. 10, October 1969

For a Silver Wedding

… and they recognised him in the breaking of bread.

Lk 24:31

Silver wedding celebrations have a lot in common with Emmaus. There's a pause on the journey, a Eucharist, a realisation that God has walked with two people. Like the two who met Christ on the road and went with him to Emmaus, these two who have walked twenty-five years together greet us on this day as witnesses to the reality of the Resurrection. They have been to Emmaus, Christ has walked with them – this day is proof – and we meet together to celebrate their meeting with each other, their meeting with Christ and their joy.

'A man I met on the road' is almost the sacrament of the accidental. Most marriages have this same quality of the accidental about them. Jean Guitton tells of a group of prisoners of war who, to pass the time, began to tell how their fathers met their mothers. 'I remember the oddest trivialities providing the circumstances: a smile, a lock of hair, a jest, a glove picked up, a lost train, a look! Our game did not go on very long before everyone became serious, awed when he realised on what a pyramid of chance he was poised.' Today they and we look back and give thanks for the chance which made them meet each other and Christ in each other. But as we look back we feel that the chance was not altogether chance but rather more the contrived accident of the road to Emmaus.

Meetings with God – in person or in people – have always something of Emmaus about them. God is present, acting and speaking, but his Incarnation in the event and circumstances is so complete that his presence is unnoticed until the last moment or afterwards. Without realising this we often recognise it in fact – because usually we thank God for something that is past, for the favour received. We are unsure of the present and do not see him with us in it. We hope he is, but, like the people he walked with to Emmaus, we are 'slow to believe'. So their silver wedding is a sign both for this couple and for us. For them, as for us, there will have been many times in their life together when they did not realise or forgot that he was with them. It is only afterwards – now – that they can look back and be sure and give thanks.

Emmaus was not just for two disciples, and for that moment; it was also for the others, and for the future. Emmaus was a pledge of the continuing Emmanuel – God with us. There is still much life to be lived. There will be again old difficulties and new hazards, but the road from Emmaus is lit with a new assurance.

In their walking together this husband and wife have, of course, known the disillusionment and the disappointment which are part of all journeys to Emmaus. They have survived temptations, casual and sudden, of monotony and loneliness and curiosity and the longing for adventure down a thousand byways. Some they have faced together and some individually but always with that other whom they met on the road. He has been with them together for a quarter of a century. These two have lived together and broken bread together for twenty-five years and they have known him in the breaking of bread.

Golden Wedding

Early in the day it was whispered that we should set sail in a boat, only thou and I, and never a soul in the world would know of this our pilgrimage to no country and to no end.

Rabindranath Tagore

Fifty years of existence in a structure so time-reliant as the union of human life and human love calls for a special sort of celebration, and for once time is not the enemy but the celebrant.

That this celebration should be called golden is mankind's tribute to its quality. No metal is mined deeper in human history and consciousness. It is and has been the object of desires and dreams, the reward of superlative achievement, the touchstone of worth, the measure of value in all our exchanges. After so long a time the hallmark may well have faded on the plain gold ring with which this man wed this woman fifty years ago. But today time itself has assayed the marriage which the ring made and marked it as genuine.

The guests on their wedding morning shared their joy. It was then the joy of a hopeful departure. We, the guests on their golden wedding morning, share their joy too but it is a different joy – the joy of an arrival and of hope fulfilled. The wishes made and the hopes expressed at wedding breakfasts seem sometimes in their exaggeration and vehemence to be tinged with fear. For we know that human happiness has a high mortality rate. So the wishes for the success of a marriage are pitched high and we tell each other what a lovely couple they are, as if with the strength of words to storm the citadels of the future. But the silent artillery of time is unfortunately not spiked by good wishes. And so part of the joy of this golden wedding is that for once our wishes have come true. It is not just one couple's triumph – it is a triumph for all of us and we have so few.

In photographs of golden wedding groups the old couple seem often to be slightly, tolerantly, amused by the fuss. We seem almost to exhibit them as trophies and they let us. They enjoy and are happy in their children's celebration of the event, but there is a secret quality to their happiness that not even their children know. Children nearly always think of their parents as existing only from the time that they have known them, but this man and this woman share times and secrets and memories that are theirs and only theirs. In Yeats's words they

... have found the best that life can give,
Companionship in those mysterious things
That make a man's soul or a woman's soul
Itself and not some other soul.

'The Gift of Harun al-Rashid', W. B. Yeats

Fifty and more years of reality and grace have been mediated to each through the other. The family has grown out of the basic unit of their marriage, but their marriage has not lost its identity in the greater family unit. It has preserved its own individual and secret being, unshared. So out of their meaning for each other, from the years that are locked away from all outsiders, they smile to each other and share their happiness with all.

Homilies for January

Vol. 38, No. 12, December 1987

Second Sunday after Christmas

Harvard, the famous American university, has 'Veritas' as its motto. You'll see the word on its T-shirt, broken into three bits. A man brought up on the classics pointed it out to me as a parable of our civilisation – the fractured truth.

'What is truth?' said Pilate jesting, and would not stay for an answer. Pilate had to turn away because truth was staring him in the face. Truth and the courts were thought to be partners once. Now nobody can be sure. We are more sceptical for we have seen too much evidence of the triumphant and profitable lie.

Today's readings are all in praise of God who is Truth – the God of wisdom, God of holiness, God of kindness who manifested himself to us in the Word who is God, that Word who was the true Light that gave light to all people.

Our words should reflect that Word, but our word has become a most dishonoured pledge. We were chosen in Christ to be holy and spotless, chosen to be the adopted children of God. But how faintly our time reflects Our Father in his truth!

The word we give in ordinary dealings is often doubtful, and people say the oath we use in court is a discredited guarantee. Our word is so often not God's. Today's readings bring up sharply the contrast between the Word and our word.

The truth has become expendable. Publicly it is at the mercy of business and politics and communications. There are times when they show it little mercy. We blame them, of course, and we distrust them. But privately and personally the lie seems to matter less – a makeweight to put with 'bad thoughts' and 'backbiting' at confessions. And we think of the lie as a matter of speech. But you can write it down, or not write it down, in a curriculum vitae or a reference or a tax return or a grant application.

And perjury? What's that?

The car was on the wrong side of the road. It never dimmed.
I was doing only thirty miles an hour. I had only one drink. I
now have a pain in my left leg day and night.

Work:	Who's getting a bad time?
	Who's giving it?
	Who makes allowances?
	Who's always in good form?
	Who has time to explain?
	Who praises work well done?
	Who dodges, and lets someone else in for it?
	Who's not too particular about honesty?
	Who's taking off the site?
	Who gives a hand?
	Who gives a damn?
Home:	Who's out every night?
	Who's never thanked?
	Who's the family scapegoat?
	Who's always looking for more than a fair share?
	Who's lied to? Who's telling the lies?
	Who's left short?
	Who always starts the argument?
Neighbours:	Who carries the story?
	Who always helps?
	Who is very touchy?
	Who is always complaining?
	Who always wants to share?
	Who thinks his/her children are perfect?
	(Please tell other parents where you get them, they'd love some too.)
	Who cares?

Is it you? See for yourself.

It's baptism time for Our Lord. Now the work of Christmas
begins.

When the song of the angels is stilled,
When the star in the sky is gone,
When the kings and princes are home,
When the shepherds are back with their flock,
The work of Christmas begins:

To find the lost, to heal the broken,
To feed the hungry, to release the prisoner,
To rebuild the nations, to bring peace among people,
To make music in the heart.

Second Sunday of the Year

Another kind of epiphany. No stars. No singing. No kings. No camels. No gold. The wise men were exceptional in that they had to travel to meet God. But even they met God in his home, and having met him they were sent home again.

Home, neighbourhood, is our meeting place with God. A distant Christ would be a contradiction of the Incarnation. The God who came is a household God – domestic, local, available, approachable, familiar. We would be wrong to expect strange epiphanies. Christ sets himself in the ordinary, in the family. Bethlehem is a place 'where all men are at home'.

Today's first reading and gospel make the point again. Samuel thinks it is the voice of his employer calling him. He mistakes the voice of God for the voice of his master, Eli. But it is Eli who directs Samuel to God, who interprets God's voice for him. It is Eli who recognises the divine and prepares Samuel for his epiphany, his meeting with God.

In our time we do not easily think of epiphany in the relation of employer and employee. We do not easily think of the divine in office or shop or at a bench. But the voice that called for a listening servant and found Samuel in the house where he worked calls still today. It looks still for listening servants – for people who will respect and help one another, for people who will be priest for one another, and mediate God to one another as Eli did for Samuel.

The workplace is one of the ordinary places of epiphany. It is to this place we must bring our everyday gifts. We are long off the gold standard, and frankincense and myrrh are long gone from the commodity market. As epiphany gifts, skill and dedication, loyalty and honesty, kindness and care, are what the hands of Christ now, working, giving work, or seeking work, reach for.

The other ordinary place of epiphany is home. Today's gospel is the epiphany of the grown Messiah. 'If you want to know me come and live with me,' is one of the commonest Irish pieces of folk wisdom. In today's gospel the very first disciples and Christ respect the validity of the phrase: 'Where do you live?' they ask. 'Come and see,' he says.

The ordinary and the familiar are both help and hindrance to our finding Christ, and recognising him. Because we are so accustomed to our own we miss Christ in them. Home is the last place you expect to find him. And he's not hidden there, only unrecognised. Because he's unrecognised there we sometimes fail to give thanks for him. But that doesn't mean he is neglected. The vast care and the constant work of the ordinary time are nothing less than the vast love and the constant kindness of Christ. Many homes that would lay no great claim to holiness are the tabernacles of the most real presence of God that can be on earth – the caring, day in, day out, in love, in sickness, in health, in age, in infancy, in adolescence, of one human being for another. It would be a pity if we missed this everyday, extraordinary epiphany just because it is so common. We should today recognise it and give thanks for it. Where do you live, Christ? Come and see. You'll find him at home.

And one last thing in today's gospel – again domestic and very ordinary and maybe very Irish. Myles na gCopaleen made a character called 'the brother' very famous – a man who knew everyone and who could get you anything, and at the right price. You have only to ask. This day's gospel wouldn't be complete without him. It is always worth remembering that Andrew met Christ first, and the next morning he told his brother Simon and brought him to Jesus. And that was how Peter met Christ – through 'the brother'. Perhaps that is parable and exemplar of how we all meet him.

Third Sunday of the Year
The good news. Christ the newscaster. Christ the net-caster.

What good news? – and our traditional herring grounds nearly fished out by foreign trawlers!

Today is 24 January 1988 and here is the news read by Fr Michael Murphy (or Fr Ned or Tim or Pat, or Don, and not necessarily Murphy).

First the headlines: Speaking in Galway the Minister for Salvation said today that the time has come and the kingdom of

God is now close at hand. The Minister for Penance says there is an urgent need to repent. People should believe the good news. Here are the details …

The above is a repeat broadcast of a bulletin first broadcast 2,000 years ago. The first broadcaster announced it as 'the good news from God'. It got a hearing – good news is scarce. It went on – he went on – 'today', 'tonight' for three years. Finally, the authorities decided it should be taken off. They killed it. Then the pirates got hold of it, Radio Mark, Radio Matthew, Luke, John, Peter, Paul – you find them everywhere you know, crowding out the bands. They broadcast it everywhere, and continuously – very high frequency you might say.

And those who are listening – well, they wonder, is it news? And is it good?

Is it news? We sometimes need to rub our eyes for two reasons: (i) to get the sleep out of them, (ii) to make sure we are really seeing what we think we see. With us and Christ we need to rub our eyes for the first reason. Our senses are dulled by familiarity, by availability. After all – bread – you can't be much more common than that. Did God sell himself too cheap to us? He's like a mother or father in a family, like a husband or wife, like a brother or sister growing up with you. It's only when they are away or gone or dead that we realise their full meaning for us – all they do (did) that we never notice (noticed). Often when they are there we are more conscious of them as irritant than we are prepared to acknowledge them as benefit. ('Why are you always nagging me?' 'I'll do my lessons when "Dallas" is over.' 'Did you get the sugar?' 'Tell the priest?' 'Send off the application form?' 'Make your bed?' 'Change your shirt?' – but 'Where are my socks?' 'Will you fix this for me?' 'I need 50p.')

We sometimes see God as an irritant, I think, a sort of celestial *Skibbereen Eagle* keeping a holy eye on us.

And Christ was at pains to tell us that his awareness of us and of our needs was the awareness of love, constant, minute, infinitely generous – even the hairs of our heads are numbered. ('Did you comb your hair?') A love rather like our mother's or our father's.

Would we miss her love if it weren't there?

Perhaps we need to rub our eyes twice – first to get the sleep out of them, and then to look in wonder at what we see. Because that was Christ's final message: it's real – 'See my hands, reach your hand here and put it into my side.'

And is it good? For people besieged by the everyday – by worry, by ill-health, by the demands of love – to know that it had a meaning and a value and was recognised gratefully by God? Is that good? For people grieving in the separation of death to know that separation is temporary and there will be a reunion in happiness and no more tears? Is that good?

For people unjustly treated to be assured of the justice of their case, to know that God did see, and that one day they would get it? For people trying to forgive and people trying to make peace and people struggling to do the right thing – to know that theirs would be the kingdom of heaven? Is that good?

Final word: I asked a missionary about to return to the country where she worked, if she thought she was good news. She had no doubt. She gave meaning and hope, she said, to women who were slaves. Sometimes literally, in an absolutely male-dominated Muslim society. They lose their sight making carpets for the Western World.

She had no doubt they longed for her return. They know she feels their pain, and she is giving them a little light, leading them to some kind of new life. So they delight in her. She had no doubt.

But she said she was 'as lonely as hell'. Incarnation, good news – it's needed, West or East, then or now. And it's real but it costs. 'See my hands. Reach your hand here and put it into my side.'

Fourth Sunday of the Year
'I can't get him to eat.' Parents often complain nowadays that children are 'picky': they'll only eat what pleases them, not what's good for them. Parents think they weren't like that and weren't allowed to be like that. But the children perhaps resemble their parents – for if the children are 'picky', the parents are 'choosy'.

At least that's one of the things some of the authorities in the Church have been talking about – the à la carte Catholic – the one who picks and chooses, who treats what the Church says or what the Pope says like the sweets display in Woolworths – the 'pick 'n' mix' mixture.

Today's world is not a good world for authority or authority figures. They get a bad press. Interestingly as the force of authority declines we become more certain of our own rightness. The demon of omniscience possesses a lot of us a lot of the time. All kinds of people on television and in the newspapers seem to be surer than – well, as sure as – the Pope. But infallibility belongs only to him, and in closely defined circumstances.

Perhaps the demon in today's gospel is that demon of 'Don't tell me. I know.' The demon shouts, 'I know who you are.' But Jesus said sharply, 'Be quiet. Come out of him.' Jesus ejects and rejects the unclean spirit who knew it all.

Certainly today's readings put God on the side of the authority that comes from himself. He promises a prophet like Moses and, 'I will put my words in the mouth of the prophet, who shall speak to them everything that I command. Anyone who does not heed the words that the prophet shall speak in my name, I myself will hold accountable' (Deut 18:18–19). That's the *vox Dei* (Voice of God).

In the gospel it's the vox populi which recognises in Christ the fulfilment of the promise voiced so long before by God. 'Here is a teaching which is new', they said, 'and with authority behind it.'

Christ, of course, vouched for the truth of what he said by his deeds.

It's the oldest test of the word – the matching deed. Fashions may change but the validity of these coordinates, word and matching deed, never do. Christ was to offer it again as the test 'By their fruits you shall know them' and he would go to his death in proof of it: 'Greater love no man has …'

The Christian life is a struggle for coordination. Tie matches shirt. Blouse matches skirt – it is more difficult to achieve deed matching word, and lips matching heart. And when we fail we sometimes blame the demander and the demand. We could meet failure with humility, and admission, and repentance. But that is to admit authority. Our present possessing demon, however, cements our certainty and makes us deny the validity of authority's claim. But authority has a place and a meaning and a value. We have that in today's readings on no less an authority than God's. Parent to child, we would admit this but, God to adult, we don't find admission easy.

Such admission is, however, only an admission that we are creatures and he is Creator, that we do depend on him, that we don't know everything, and that he loves us and we can trust him. It's not such a burden, but when we refuse to carry it we often have to assume the much heavier burdens of anger, and the consequences of failure to follow the truth. Because that is essentially what God's authority is proclaiming – the truth. The Ten Commandments are rooted in reality and truth – the truth of fact about God, the truth of psychology, the truths of relationship. A world where there isn't stealing (or any of its relations with fancier names), where there isn't adultery, where there is respect for people and marriage, where there is respect for life, is the best kind of world. That's fairly easy to see and to admit. Our trouble seems to be that like St Paul we find it easy to agree but hard to do and that, unlike St Paul, we resent being told. But it may help to remember that God tells us these things because they are true. He is not just imposing arbitrary strictures to test obedience.

In temper of the present time, however, we do resent being told. 'My private affairs', 'My personal life' – we resent all intruders into these and God gets reduced to the rank of intruder, and a very disturbing one.

But today's readings make clear the place and importance he gives to authority, and the use it has for, and strength it gives to, both the teacher and the taught. We must beware of being unable to see or accept the truth because it comes as a commandment rather than as a suggestion. Because that's what God gave, what Moses taught, what Christ stood for – the Ten Commandments, not the ten suggestions.

Easter Sunday

Faced with a worn text on a Saturday night a man will often ask himself, 'What can one say about that that's new? It has all been said before.' The problem does not arise about the Easter sermon because one does not have to say anything new. Some few truths in human history and experience lie outside the range of time's silent artillery. They remain always startling and un-shattered.

Easter is like this. It is beyond the power of the cliché. 'He is not here for he has risen, as he said he would.' Death has ceded to life and the one promise on which the destiny of all men, before and after, hung has been kept, 'as he said he would'.

The history of mankind's sorrows is a history of broken promises – from Eden to the newest war, the latest divorce. But no defeat is final and all disasters are retrievable because this one promise has been kept, 'for he has risen, as he said he would'.

In *De Profundis* Oscar Wilde quoted a Greek aphorism, 'Even the gods cannot alter the past', and he commented 'Christ showed that the commonest sinner could do it, that it was the one thing he could do.' We can do it because Christ has done it. He altered the past and shaped the future by his Resurrection. The decree against us was nailed to the cross with him – our past was set at nought – and his Resurrection gives us a future that is nothing less than glorious. When Christ rose from the dead the power of God was validated and we were set free.

The Resurrection gives validity to all our sacraments and each of them shares its influence over time, past, present or future; time the servant of eternity. Baptism which makes us like Christ is each man's personal resurrection and, like Christ's, it stretches back to the beginning of mankind and forward to the end of time. For each of us our baptism goes, like his Resurrection, as far back as the first sin and is unfinished work until we rise glorious from the dead. Penance is the sacrament of the continuous past and immediate future. The Eucharist is the sacrament of the continuous present. The last anointing reaches backwards and forwards. Confirmation and matrimony and holy orders are sacraments of the future.

In the gospel accounts – even beyond the sense of the words – we can feel the freedom and expansion of the Resurrection. Like a well-lit play, the Passion begins with the closing of a door 'and it was night'. Man the betrayer goes off alone in the dark. The action proceeds through claustrophobic courtroom and hilltop, and all the earth grows dark. The final act on Sunday begins with the opening of a tomb: 'toward dawn', says Matthew; 'just as the sun was rising', says Mark; 'at the first sign of dawn', says Luke.

It is all symbolic of a freedom conferred on us this day. Even we the commonest sinners can now alter the past and shape the future. For this Christ rose, 'the first born of many brothers'.

Second Sunday of Easter

Brendan Behan is said to have remarked once as he chaired a meeting of fellow Irishmen, 'The first item on the agenda is a split.' It is fair comment on human affairs and true far away from Ireland.

The account of the early days of Christianity given in today's first reading is a sort of parable to show us what the Resurrection aimed at doing and could do for people. The original community of the human race is restored. The Christians pray together, own everything in common, share their food gladly and generously and are looked up to by everyone. One can sense the happiness that comes from unity, generosity and community.

That is chapter two of the Acts. By chapter six – the reading for the Fifth Sunday of Easter – 'The Hellenists made a complaint against the Hebrews. In the daily distribution their own widows were being overlooked.' Groups within the community have resumed their identity. The serpent of division has appeared as he always will.

His appearance, however, is not what matters – what matters is his victory if it occur. The Resurrection does not promise his non-appearance, it offers the possibility of his defeat at any time and the certainty of his final defeat. Here the apostles solved their distribution problem in the most modern manner by forming a limited company responsible for distribution, the seven deacons.

The struggle of the Resurrection is always against the divisive serpent who first set wife against husband, and men against God. In today's Christendom, enlarged and complex, the warmth and closeness of that early community is not always possible. The serpent is often size, distance, number. It is not as easy to feel united with, to give gladly and generously to, people we do not see, but if our mission as aides to the Risen Christ is to be accomplished, if we are to heal the wounded community, it is still our task 'to give gladly and generously'.

But where are the seven deacons? Perhaps we should see the State as today's universal diaconate – the means through which we help those 'whose silence is heard only of God'. It is one of the main agencies through which we must restore that original community.

The more fully Christian we are then, the easier it must become to pay taxes – at least we may be able to see it as no longer extortion but gift. Today's reading is not just a sentimental recall of the Church's golden age, the days that were and never will be more. It demands action. Christ gave not just pity but food to the hungry crowd, not just consolation but cure to those who were sick, not just guidance, but sight to the blind. The early Christians shared out the proceeds among themselves, according to what each one needed. No less is asked of us – the examples we have are not just the ideal of Christianity but the reality. If the aged and the outcasts are to have warmth and food, if the widows and the deserted are not to continue complaining, if the homeless are to have homes and the sick to have treatment, perhaps we should be campaigning to have our income tax increased. What actually happens is the sort of rejoicing and self-congratulation which took place when the English government reduced income tax by a couple of pence. Today's story of those who shared gladly and generously is not just a remembrance but a reminder.

Third Sunday of Easter
There is an odd description of God in St Peter's first letter: 'Your Father, one who has no favourites.' We have a saying, 'There's favouritism in hell.' Putting these two statements together maybe hell is the natural habitat of favouritism.

André Malraux tells in one of his books of a French general who had been liberated from one of the Nazi prison camps. When Malraux met him, 'he said to me superciliously "of course they didn't put us in with the people in stripes"' – the ordinary prisoners who wore striped clothes. What is one to do faced with our notions of ourselves and what they reveal about us? Malraux comments wearily, 'Slaps soon fade and one man can only shrug two shoulders.'

We live in a world where is a lot of favouritism. We call it different names: influence, pull, bribery, graft, backhand, unfair use of information. Whatever name we call it, it puts some people in an unfair privileged position and it is not God's doing. A lot of it can fit aptly under 'injustice'. There are times when people, ordinary people, feel it all round them, feel cynical about their country, and opposed to the belief that there is much that is venal and corrupt in state life. Many shoulders are shrugged.

St Peter points out the fairness of God and says we must be like him, scrupulously careful. Our ransom was not paid with anything corruptible, but with the blood of Christ. He rose from the dead, keeping his promise for our sake, 'so that you would have faith and hope in God'.

The people who have the sharpest eye for favouritism of any kind – in family, in school, in world – are the young. In the beginning they often protest and then they settle down in disillusionment when they discover that their world or country is run on two systems, one overt for public acknowledgment, the other the covert world of the private deal, the inner ring, the spoils system. When we sometimes wonder why young people lack faith and hope in God we should remember that that must be given them through faith and hope in people.

In the end they will have what we give them – faith and hope in 'a word in the right quarter'. They will become like us, feel helpless, acquiesce in the system, support it and use it.

Is this sort of world fair to another class of people, those who don't know 'someone'? Who don't know where you can get it wholesale, who must often buy on hire purchase and pay even more than the retail price? Is there a continuing violence done to the un-influential and the poor by a vast, cosy, middle class club?

Does a shapeless but real freemasonry of the better-off classes afflict the poorer outside groups? Their vague awareness of the second system into which they cannot break finally crystallises in disturbance and then we are frightened. We forget that the fault may be ours, for we have hidden Christ from them and denied them faith and hope in God.

Fourth Sunday of Easter
We were in a queue waiting outside a dining-car on the Dublin train. It wasn't a big queue – five people – and it had broken down into a group, chatting amiably, still far from Dublin, knowing we had lots of time, and that it wouldn't be long until we got into the restaurant car anyway. A happy group – explaining why we hadn't brought our cars. 'A man'd be a fool … God, when ye see th'accidents …' One man was doing most of the talking – nothing special about him, good-natured, corroborating our experiences, filling in the last words of our sentences, causing and leading most of the laughter. Good-natured you'd say, except that whenever a waiter appeared – it happened three times – he suddenly changed, and each time complained loud and long about the delay. 'What's the meaning of this … no wonder losing money … paying passengers … rights of citizens.' And immediately the waiter left he subsided into good nature again. He was in no hurry at all and perfectly happy. But the third time somebody in the group, half-embarrassed, remonstrated. 'Ah, sure there's lots of time … maybe doing their best … like.' His answer was good humoured as ever. 'Ah, I know, I know, but my policy is, boy – it's the screechin' wheel that gets the oil, it's the screechin' wheel that gets the oil.'

There are moments when we seem to live in a world of 'screechin' wheels'. Good causes are being devalued because protests have become so numerous. Reaction (or its big brother, backlash) is expected to every situation, and all our senses are assaulted by its frequency on radio, television and newspaper. The media have prospered from reaction. 'What is your reaction to?' 'Asked what his reaction was he said …'

Today's reading can hardly be popular – it counsels not answering back, not showing reaction, putting up with, having patience. It simply says this is the way Christ was – 'He was insulted …

and did not retaliate with insults.' In present times one is almost ashamed to suggest that it might be good not to answer back – but there is little doubt that Christ is being held up for our admiration and imitation. We cannot interpret our way out of it despite the poor market for patience.

Perhaps at least we need reminding that the protest isn't always the answer – in our smaller concerns anyway. In our homes, between husband and wife, between neighbours, between friends, patience can be the better part of wisdom and sanctity.

The kind of patience Christ showed has become so unfashionable that it is totally misunderstood. It is given other names that are hard to bear, and how often we advise against it. 'Well, I wouldn't take it from him, her, them.' 'Don't let him, her, them, walk over you.' And so often what was a border incident escalates into full-scale war.

Today we are shown the difficulty of being Christian and perhaps also its glory. Alain once said, speaking of Christ, 'The slap on the face takes the form of the man who receives it, not the one who gives it.' If we react in kind – the backlash – we make one kind of situation; if we do not react we make another kind of situation. In which, think you, would you find Christ?

Fifth Sunday of Easter
When it mattered to me, the best sort of algebra book to have was the one with the answers in the back. There was the one without the answers – it was cheaper – but at the end of the exercise it failed to give any security. But even with the answers you still had, of course, to work out the problem. The fact that Mr Hall or Mr Knight had years before worked it out to their satisfaction did not make your work less rough, but it did give you the comfort of knowing that you were right.

Maybe in a way it spoiled us, and made us uneasy later in life, when there was no readymade answer or no way we could check our answer. Lots of people became too dependent on instant answers – is it a sin or isn't it – and our theologies of injustice or fasting, for instance, often shaded into the world of Maxwell Smart – would you believe £5, or two ounces?

Perhaps we can recognise ourselves and find some comfort in today's gospel. After three years with Christ the Apostles still have unanswered questions, and Philip says, 'Lord, let us see the Father and we shall be satisfied.' They are still looking for the one complete answer at the back of the book – even though Christ had told a parable once to point out that there was no answer like that in this life. 'Ah, but if someone were to come back from the dead they would believe.' ... And he had answered they wouldn't believe then either, and he proved it by rising from the dead to a continuing storm of disbelief. As the American poet wrote a few years ago, he is

> according to a round-up of late world news
> from the usual unreliable sources
> real dead.

> 'A Coney Island of the Mind',
> Lawrence Ferlinghetti

In our anxiety for an answer to our problems and the world's we have all tried and seen different solutions – possessions, drugs, power, other creeds, other persons. Today Christ says simply that he is the answer. 'I am the way, and the truth, and the life.'

The answer is easy but the solution is not. We still have to do the working out. Getting to know Christ cannot be so easy – else he would not have had to say sadly to Philip, 'Have I been with you all this time, Philip, and you still do not know me?' Getting to know Christ, which is getting to know the will of his Father, is rarely simple in concrete situations. We can readily enough see that if all men really loved their neighbours very many of the world's problems would be solved. But for the parent faced with a son in his dark years, or the people in a marriage shaken by drink, or selfishness or infidelity, or in a million other minor domestic tragedies or decisions, the way is not clear and the working out is slow and painful. Knowing Christ and being like him in these situations is travelling the narrow road.

Is there naught for our consolation then? For once there is an answer – Christ's remark to his lonely and disturbed disciples. 'Do not let your hearts be troubled. Trust in God and trust in me.' His nearness to us, his sympathy in today's reading, and his power – these are the factors present in all our situations which can change these situations. We have become so aware of him as man that we sometimes forget that he is also God. Said by us these words would be empty but these are the words of God, invested with his power. Do we believe them? There is only one answer to this question, and it is each man's own.

Homilies for April

Vol. 34, No. 3, March 1983

Easter Sunday

Easter Sunday morning is not one on which you expect long sermons and the first good news is that you won't be disappointed – it's not a day for penance and there's no point in continuing Lent into Easter.

But, as we say, I couldn't let the occasion pass, because this is the one occasion that makes sense of all the others. We celebrate today mankind's greatest hour – no moment in history is as momentous as Easter. For us clay creatures, made from the earth, and destined for the earth, Easter is the earth shattering event. The tomb opened from the inside and now there's no holding us. Not even the sky is our limit.

This is the feast that defeats all our symbols of defeat – the hat you flung at it, the towel you throw in, the given up ghost, the last nail in the coffin, the last straw, the whole damned thing. Easter reverses the charges, settles the debt, opens the prison, picks us off our knees and raises the hand of man in victory.

> Death with life contended
> Combat strangely ended
> Life's own champion slain yet lives to reign.

> *The Beauty of the Cross:*
> *The Passion of Christ in Theology and the Arts,*
> *from the Catacombs to the Eve of the Renaissance,*
> Richard Viladesau

Christmas is for giving, and Whit is for inspiration, and Lent for licking into shape but they're all just roads leading to or from – where? Nowhere – if Easter didn't happen. They're all dependencies of Easter. Why rejoice at Christmas, why deprive at Lent, why gird at Pentecost or celebrate Our Lady or the saints? If there is no Easter there's nothing to celebrate. We're still winter and summer solstice people, equinox pagans in the dark about God – if there's no Easter. The gospels are wishful thinking, and the sanctuary lamp flickers foolishly – if Christ is not risen.

The great cathedrals and the little churches are as meaningless as each other if there's no Easter. Notre Dame is not only misnamed but a monument to the misled. And St Paul's and St Patrick's and St Peter's and all their lesser brethren are built on flawed foundations. They become symbols not of hope but of wish, standing for a sad unreality.

And not just buildings but people, us, – for we are all children of Easter, dependants of a risen Christ. If he is not risen, said St Paul, we are the most unfortunate of people. And the long obituary lists in the paper are indeed the final roll call and the grief there is in every named home knows no cure. The tear will flow to dry only in the dust; no one will wipe it away.

And even our names are devalued; what's in a Christian name, if there's no Easter? For there's no saint and Mary Anne and John and Michael Joe might as well be called Athene and Jupiter and Crom Cruach. And Thomas is not just doubtful but doomed if there's no Easter.

But there is Easter and that's why the bells ring and the organ plays and the *Gloria* returns. That's why the words of the Mass – the sober Mass – go a little mad with joy. Almost as if the Church was throwing its hands in the air and shouting 'We won'. Listen to the man in the responsorial psalm.

> The Lord's right hand has triumphed
> His right hand raised me up
> I shall not die, I shall live to tell the story.

And we answer back: 'This day was made by the Lord, we rejoice and are glad.'

Christ is risen, we won. That's the real good news. And the bad news? The good news is that finally there's no bad news – because Easter happened. So that's why I couldn't let the occasion pass.

Happy Easter.

Second Sunday of Easter

If there's a God don't we treat him very badly? I mean if there's someone who made this world, made us and will in the end judge what we made of ourselves and our lives – if he exists, if it's true, doesn't he get fairly miserable recognition from us? A Sunday nod of the head, maybe a morning wave of the hand – sometimes the back of it. Did it ever strike you that we treat God a bit like a child, as if he were the child and we the adults? 'Don't bother me now … Will you stop asking questions? … Can't you see I'm busy? … I will later if you're good … Are you still up? … No I don't love you any more … Didn't I ask you to …? … Will you stop talking and stay quiet? … Go out and play', and ungraciously we do give him a look-in sometimes! 'Oh all right so, here you are – but I don't want to hear another word from you for the rest of the week' … 'I have enough bother without you.' Not fully true, maybe, but near enough. Does God ever realise how inconvenient he can be?

Were you surprised that I said 'if there's a God'? Well I was trying to talk to the atheist in you. Oh, you're not an atheist? Ever? What about me? you ask. Yes, me too. There are a lot of lives we lead where God does not exist, or where we deny him existence. Is God always alive and well in your business life, in your sexual life, in your family life, in your speech, in the way you deal with insurance, in the way you pay your income tax? 'Oh God', 'Oh no'.

At certain times and places he is an embarrassment. Don't bring him into the supermarket, into the office; keep him out of the public house, out of the garage. Keep him in the church – he's safe there. Well, it's his house, isn't it? Aren't ye always preaching that people should stay at home more?

If there's a God – well, would you believe it? Would anybody believe it if they saw us anywhere but in the church? How are you on providing evidence?

I think today's gospel of doubt is written for our time. We're more inclined now to doubt and to deny – we're not so inclined to accept responsibility. A girl wrote about New York as a city and said, 'Here it doesn't matter whether you win or lose – it's where you lay the blame.' We're all New Yorkers; we don't want blame. Time was people said 'Your disobedient servant' – and went to confession. Now we often absolve ourselves – mustn't let God get too close to us – by saying 'there's no sin'.

If there's no God there's no sin – and we are today in danger of reversing the argument and saying if there's no sin there's no God. We make the real unreal and the unreal real. At best he becomes an it-doesn't-matter-anyway God. Like an aging boxer or footballer who has hung on too long, he becomes just a pale shadow of his former self. Past glory. So the lie gets substituted for the truth and the world stumbles along through massacres, and robberies and wars, and we through humble adulteries and petty thefts and small falsities.

Existence goes topsy-turvy and we need more police because instead of protecting one another, we must be protected from one another. And we think we can deny God except in church and safely ignore him everywhere else. And who needs confession when there's no sin – only crimes and complexes?

But I'm not waving a banner this morning which says 'Bring back God.' He's never far away. When we close our eyes or our minds he doesn't go out of existence – thank God. When we dress up and play God as children play house and mummies and daddies, he doesn't get mad and abandon us. No, he's always about and very near and loves us still.

That's why this morning's gospel is so valuable to us who sometimes find God unreal, who sometimes pretend he doesn't exist, and yet need him so badly. There's a man in that gospel who doesn't believe, and a God who says 'Come here and touch me' and the man touches and says 'My God'. May his exclamation be our prayer this morning, may God touch us and we touch him in the Mass, and in the people we meet this day. That's after all why this story was written down by the man who wrote it: he was thinking of us. May his prayer and hope be true for you, for he said about the story, 'These are recorded so that you may believe that Jesus is the Christ, the Son of God, and that believing you may have life through his name.' I can wish no more for you or for myself.

Third Sunday of Easter
You'd have to be there to write that gospel. It starts off with a lot of men hanging round. They had lived through a lot. It was just after Easter Sunday – the first one.

I'd say they were tired talking about the last three years and Calvary and the Resurrection. Like a match that you replay in talk with the lads, every kick of it until you're tired of it. Like a death that you tell to your friends, minute by minute – when the pain became bad, what the doctor said, the last time she spoke, the final minutes, the end. And you go over it again and again. I'd say the disciples were like that , Peter and Thomas, Nathaniel in from Cana, James, John (like a writer noticing details for this morning's gospel) and a couple of others.

The talk died. Getting late in the evening, each man wrapped in his own thoughts. All of them still wondering. They had seen Christ twice since he rose but was it real, was it over, were they just dreaming? You know the way the dark brings doubt.

They had left everything to follow him. And now, what were they after it all? Nothing. Former boatman. Ex-fishermen. Time on their hands, no work, silent, somebody kicked a stone. Suddenly Peter could stand it no longer. He said 'I'm going fishing' and it has the sound of a man who's saying 'The rest of ye can come or stay as ye want.' He heads for the shore and a boat. The rest say 'Right' – glad of some decision, some action. Occupational therapy maybe but at least nets and boats and water were real. And fish were, and worth money if you could catch them.

And the night wore on and the nets went out and the nets came in and no fish. But at least they could take this sort of waiting and frustration. They were brought up to it and you kept hoping. Patience, you learned.

Then the dawn came, light over the lake. Somebody on the shore shouting as men always will to fishermen, 'Did ye catch anything?' And the short answer of disappointment – 'No.' And then the man shouts, 'Put the net out to starboard' – he sounds like someone who knows a bit about boats anyhow – 'Put the net out to starboard and you'll get something.'

Maybe he can see something moving in the water. At any rate they do and catch the full of the net – 153 – they counted them later. And they shout and haul and John turns to look at the man on the shore – a man who has a way of seeing things or is it a way with fish? 'Peter,' he said 'It's the Lord.' And Peter, who's stripped to the waist and working, turns, sees, grabs his jacket and jumps into the water to go ashore.

Everything's changed – doubts gone, dark gone, doom gone. Everything's light bright, sure. Everything's changed. But what's really changed? – just that Christ is present. But – they needed to know, especially Peter, especially us! – that he was present also when they couldn't see him; he was just as aware of them then. He didn't happen by accident to be just there just then. They were always in his thoughts. Absence doesn't remove him.

And so he tells Peter three times, 'Feed my lambs, look after my sheep, feed my sheep.' Peter starts out the night unemployed, and finishes as a man with a mission, started out with time on his hands and finishes with eternity on his hands.

And Christ reminded Peter of the night before – Peter striding out strong to the water, 'I'm going fishing.' 'You put on your own belt', said Christ 'and walked where you liked. It's easy to be young.' 'But', said Christ, 'there will be other times, bad times when you won't go – you'll be made go.' He was, says John, telling Peter the kind of death he would die. But he was telling Peter more than that. He was saying, 'Don't forget last night. You thought I wasn't even real, that I was gone and that you were forgotten. It wasn't so last night and it won't be true any night; I'm with you always.'

You think he was talking only to Peter? And that John was writing that for his diary? And that Christ wasn't teaching us sheep something too? Oh but sheep are such slow learners.

Fourth Sunday after Easter
What's all the excitement about in the first reading? It's like the Sunday papers, with meetings, politics, jealousies, lies, contradictions, rejections, demands and expulsions. Here are rows and rabble rousing and, in the middle of this very Middle Eastern racket and hubbub and hustle, there are people preaching salvation and others thanking God for it. A bit like the Sunday papers, with terrible disclosures and gory details complete with pictures. Almost as if the world never changes – excited crowds on the edge of violence in Lebanon or Iran. But it wasn't quite like that. Let me explain.

Do you think you'll die? Oh, I know you know you'll die – but do you think you'll die? What do you feel this minute? Do you think that you with your mind remembering last night, or wondering about the girl in front of you or annoyed at the child distracting you, you thinking about the dinner or rocketing the ball into the back of the net or worried about the price of shoes or the cattle – do you think you'll die? Can you imagine yourself gone out of existence?

Now look at the people round you. Do you think they'll die? Can you imagine them gone out of existence? You can?

Usually we feel that we ourselves are immortal. We cannot believe in our own deaths, but we easily accept that others will die.

And the truth is that we're right about ourselves and wrong about others. You'll never go out of the existence and they won't either. So be careful, you're sitting among immortals.

That's what the excitement was about in Antioch. People were just getting the message from the disciple – it was true what they had felt all along. There was another life and it was forever and it was for everybody. It was possible, it would happen 'and the pagans were happy to hear this and they thanked the Lord for his message'.

Now don't get the idea that the people who were so happy to hear this were strange, ignorant, far-off people who wouldn't understand the sophisticated likes of you or me, and the complicated world we live in. Remember they were ordinary people living in our sort of world of riots and roguery – as I said, the world you'll be reading about in the papers this morning. Even in today's gospel when Our Lord is talking about eternal life, he twice talked about people stealing – 'no one will ever steal them from me', 'no one can steal from the Father.' Oh it's the real world all right, thieves and trickery and eternal life, an odd combination. But then I suppose, salvation and thieves – it was almost a prophetic connection – didn't the Saviour die between two thieves?

What is this salvation and eternal life they're talking about and that got the likes of you and me so excited and delighted? Well whatever it is, it is meant for ordinary people and it is not for any small number or exclusive club or country. 'A huge number', says St John; 'flocks of them', said Our Lord. You couldn't count them, says John, people from everywhere, every country, every colour – liquorice allsorts.

And they, we, are being promised a new life. It will be a different kind of life: there will be no end, no more death. It will be a different quality of life – the pains and aches gone from old bones and sad minds and grieving hearts. The hungers will be gone and the violence gone and all tears wiped away forever.

And more than all that. Each one of us has a feeling, an inner vision which is secret because often we don't even have words for it. It is a feeling of the kind of person we would like to be, that we could be if … if we got the chance, if we had the courage or the willpower. We know that there are the seeds of a finer, greater person in us. It would be us at our very best, kind and strong and calm – us at the limits of our best possibilities.

Could it ever happen? Christ says this morning, 'Yes – that's what I'm offering, what I'm promising.' That's what eternal life is – everybody at his best forever. Marvellous, wouldn't it be? No wonder the pagans were happy.

But then the cold wind comes in. Pie in the sky. It could never happen, it couldn't happen to me, it's unbelievable.

I saw a film lately about a colony of people who lived underwater for forty years. Their ship sank in the Second World War and they had lived in an air bubble a thousand feet under the sea. The ones who had been born during the forty years had no idea of the world above the water. Then one day rescuers arrive, and one of the rescuers, a young man, immediately falls in love with one of the girls. He begins to tell her about a world she has never seen – about green fields and the blue sky and the sun shining in it, something yellow and bright, warm and lighting the whole world. To her it sounded like a dream. She could not even imagine it. Pie in the sky, you might say, except that she didn't even know what a sky was.

This was what her rescuer promised her, and because he was good, and because he loved her and she loved him, she believed him. Was she right to? Or should she have doubted and turned away?

Isn't it a little bit like our own story? Someone who came to save us, and love us, and promises us new life.

That's what we just read of in the gospel: 'And Jesus said: the sheep that belong to me listen to my voice. I give them eternal life. They will never be lost.'

Hey, are you listening?
Is there someone speaking to me?

Homilies for May

Vol. 25, No. 4, April 1974

Fourth Sunday of Easter

Maybe it was the fact that Paul and Barnabas were expelled from Antioch which made me think of Solzhenitsyn. He wrote back to Russia what Paul might well have written back to Antioch: 'So that the country and people do not suffocate, and so that they all have the chance to develop and enrich us with ideas, allow competition on an equal and honourable basis – not for power but for truth – between all ideological and moral currents, in particular between all religions.'

The problems of today's people of God are often the problems of the people of God in the infant Church. They were presented, as we are, with a mission.

> I have set you to be a light for the Gentiles,
> so that you may bring salvation to the ends of the earth.
>
> Acts 13:47

We were all, from then to now, chosen to be a band of saviours led by Christ. Many refuse(d) the mission, many accept(ed) it doubtfully. The choice for them and us is still between power and truth, and many of us become more concerned with power. We refuse to be the light, we want to be the one who throws the switch and controls the light.

The Church – and its individual members – like all institutions and all human beings, is faced always with the temptation of power – conquer first and impose your own truth. Well, trade may follow the flag, but faith doesn't and truth doesn't. We have been chosen to show Christ to the nations and our neighbour. When we substitute ourselves we are guilty of betrayal and blasphemy – for only Christ can say: 'I am the truth.'

The substitution of ourselves, the imposition of our own truth can only hide Christ and make our mission a failure. One of the stories from the Spanish conquest of South America makes the point: there was a native king who would not renounce his religion and was about to be burned at the stake. As the fire blazed up around him he was for the last time offered baptism. He refused, because he was afraid, he said, that if he agreed he might 'go to heaven, and meet there only Christians'.

'So,' said Paul, 'we must turn to the pagans.' Our saviours are often unlikely ones – a carpenter for us all, a farm girl for France, a slave boy for Ireland. They share another characteristic – they are not recognised at the time. Even at a more local and personal level we do not recognise our saviours. They are quite unlikely and they often wear disguises. They may be those of our own household, disguised as husband, or wife, or child. They may be outsiders disguised by something that distracts us because we don't like it – their kind of clothes, their kind of politics, their kind of accent. And you know what happens – we don't listen – give a dog a bad name, give the truth a wrong hairstyle. But we should be listening for the truth, even the partial truth of what the different voices say.

We shouldn't be so surprised about this. Christ chose us all to be a band of saviours led by him. Even you. Saviours are always unlikely.

Fifth Sunday of Easter

'They put fresh heart into the disciples' – in astonishment we might ask 'Did they need it? So soon!' After all the Lord had been lately on earth, with them; the Church had burst upon the scene with Pentecostal miracles. And already Paul and Barnabas are putting fresh heart into the disciples and 'encouraging them to persevere in the faith'.

We can understand why we might need it, two thousand years later, in a culture where AD could stand for year of the Lord or for anti-depressant. But they? Yes, they. The presence of God fades so easily in us all.

Then, as now, people faced 'the nightmare in which existence presents a face of vacancy or derision', in which faith is a folly or a scandal, in which hope is the cry of despair. 'We all have to experience many hardships,' said Paul and Barnabas, 'before we enter the kingdom of God.'

Being a Christian was always an exercise in brinkmanship – but then nobody ever said it was a broad road. It constantly juxtaposed loneliness, failure, betrayal with glory. Look at the beginning of today's gospel – 'When Judas had gone Jesus said: "Now has the Son of Man been glorified".' Betrayal and glory in one breath.

Persevering in the faith, even for St Thérèse, was sometimes dicing with doubt. She, and those first Christians of today's reading, and we the latest on the scene – we would all see ourselves in the Christ who, in the play, looks at the cross and says: 'Ah, you should have remained a tree and I should have stayed a carpenter.'

We have the ills of the first Christians and Paul and Barnabas are a long time gone back to Antioch. Where can we get that fresh heart? The answer is, of course, that we must be Paul and Barnabas to each other. Hope is not self-sustaining, it must be kindled and kept burning by love. That is one of the reasons for the demand in today's gospel: 'I give you a new commandment, love one another.'

Doctors when speaking of a drug sometimes say it has a wide or narrow range. To cure all our ills you'd need a remedy with a range as wide as the world, but listen – 'The one sitting on the throne spoke: "Now I am making the whole Creation new," he said.'

Sixth Sunday of Easter

Paul blazes through the Middle East of the first century, from one trouble spot to another, rather as Dr Kissinger does today. He was suspect in Jerusalem and he had, you remember, some trouble in Damascus. In this day's reading it might indeed be Dr Kissinger – there is disagreement in Antioch. Paul has a long argument with these men, and then he is on his way to talks in Jerusalem. The parallel, of course, cannot be pressed too far – we do not know if Dr Kissinger was ever stoned, or was often in fastings. But the coincidence of both men and the Middle East and travel and troubleshooting is enough. And for both, the quest was the same – peace.

The problems Paul and Barnabas went to Jerusalem to settle are problems no longer, but the disturbed Christians on whose behalf they were acting are still with us. We are still disturbed and, if not over the same problems, yet for the same reasons – we hear conflicting voices and we are saddled with burdens.

The realisation of this dissolves time and makes us kin with those first-century Christians. We feel their confusion in our own nerve-ends, and we learn something about our Church – that our shared disturbance is caused by and contributes to the development of the Church's teaching and the clarification of the Church's ideas.

But their problems mean little to us – an interesting historical sidelight, no more. That, too, tells us something about our Church – that the things that exercise so much disagreement today, and cause such confusion, may be an interesting historical sidelight to a Christian two hundred years from now – nothing more. History may help us to put some of our problems in perspective and not saddle ourselves with any burden 'except these essentials'. And this may give us a new courage and wisdom, and the peace which the gospel promises today.

Meanwhile they are our problems and they are not solved. Our agonies, however, our thoughts, our prayers, and our Pauls and Barnabases, are even now contributing to their solution. And the Holy Spirit is still working with us.

With His help and this morning's picture of the early Church our hearts may be less troubled and less afraid.

Seventh Sunday of Easter

There are plenty of people prepared to forgive. What we are really short of is people prepared to be forgiven. We find it hard to admit we are wrong and even harder to have it pointed out to us.

That's why Stephen's trial began calmly with the judge asking: 'Are these charges true?' – calmness comes easy to the judge. By the time the speech from the dock is over, the roles have been reversed and his judges 'began to gnash their teeth at him'.

The outrageous claim has met the outraged people and they proceed to kill Stephen. Prophets are always disturbers and then or now we want to be rid of them. We try to kill them, then by stones, now by stone deafness, but still the voice will cry out in the wilderness, grating on the edges of our comfort.

The faith that moves mountains or sees heaven thrown open is a shocking thing. It breaks down our protecting walls, it questions our foundations. We are naked in its light. It annihilates our bank balances and makes a nonentity of the Mercedes. It shows the worthlessness of our investments and our values, and so, as in any stock market crash, it causes panic.

Faith like Stephen's is a form of death. The yacht, the Riviera villa are of no value to their owner when he is on the point of death – time is a component of all material value. Remove the owner's time, as death does, and all his possessions are valueless.

Faced with faith that sees heaven open, we are suddenly off the gold standard, off every standard except that of him 'who is Alpha and Omega' and who decides 'the reward to be given to every man according to what he deserves'. That's why we shout out and stop our ears and rush at the prophet – we are fighting for our life, our kind of life.

When we hear the story of Stephen's death we are on Stephen's side because he is one of us, we think. But perhaps that's only because we see the incident as a contest. It is Christian versus Jew, and we cheer for Stephen just as we tend to support the Catholic boxer or the Catholic athlete. Old loyalties die hard and battles long ago are not easily forgotten. So we tend to identify with Stephen.

The reality may be different. Our real spiritual home – the one we live in and for – may be among the people who killed him. A real live Stephen in our midst might embarrass any of us. Because if the full truth about us were told we might be more part of the world that has not known the righteous one than of any other world.

Homilies for May

Vol. 29, No. 4, April 1978

Ascension Thursday

The story is told that a hundred years ago shopkeepers in a Scottish town ordered a cargo of oranges from Spain. They arrived, from Seville, but not the sort that had been ordered. They were small and sour. The shopkeepers refused to take them. They wouldn't stand the journey back. They were going to be taken out to sea and dumped.

Then a local woman bought them – cheap – and chopped up the rind and got rid of the pith and extracted the juice, and put a pound of sugar to a pint of liquid. Her name was Mrs Keiller and the town was Dundee. And she made marmalade. She became rich and Dundee became famous. What might have been a small tragedy became a triumph.

Calamity is only a corner on the road. I think that at the moment of the ascension, none of the Apostles would have imagined that a day would come when people would stop work and come together to celebrate what must have been to them a huge sorrow. It must have seemed to them a disaster. There they stood, looking at the empty sky – like people at a station when the train's gone out – there's no place to go now but away.

Indeed, that's what Christ had told them: 'Go, therefore, make disciples of all nations.' It seemed impossible and it was no comfort. Yet, if they looked back this was the moment when they took over the kingdom of God on earth. The memory of it, of their feelings then, must have prepared them to face other disasters later on, and to realise that calamity is only a corner on the road. We celebrate today what was originally a calamity.

Appalling things happen to people, tragic deaths and great troubles within families. Everything seems at an end, the blows are too great, too heavy – nobody could recover. But people do, and looking back we begin to see that what we thought was an ending was really a beginning.

The Holy Spirit's gift of wisdom is part of holiness, and very often that wisdom is a new vision, a new way of seeing things. In great troubles and in undeserved tragedies we often ask: 'Why?' And we complain about the absence of God, or feel he doesn't care. 'Why did God let it happen? It's hard to believe there's a God ...' Looking back, years later, like the Apostles, when things have changed and people have overcome catastrophe we can say: 'Well, isn't it remarkable?' forget that God works miracles quietly, and that we claim his absence quickly and fail to remember that he is always with us.

A man with a handicapped child told me he asked a woman with a severely handicapped child, who was now a few years old: 'Would you like to have him cured now?' And she thought and answered: 'Ah, sure, I wouldn't like to change him now.' Aren't people marvellous? Where does such strength and wisdom and goodness come from? Holiness is a new way of seeing things and calamity is only a corner on the road.

The second reading today begins with a long prayer. It's a prayer that God may help us to see through sorrows and separations, that he may give us a spirit of wisdom and perception. Then we will have greater courage and super-hope. We will know that God keeps his promises. There is nothing that can happen to us that is in the end disaster, because he is our Father, the Lord of heaven and earth.

So we celebrate today what the Apostles saw as a great sorrow and the end of cherished hopes. For what looked like an end was a beginning, what looked like a going away, absence forever, was really the very opposite – eternal presence. 'And,' said Christ, 'know that I am with you always; yes, to the end of time.'

Seventh Sunday of Easter

Honesty is the best policy – so don't cheat. All is not gold that glistens – so don't trust. He who hesitates is lost – so don't sit there, do something. Look before you leap – so don't just do something, sit there.

Proverbs are cautionary tales, stony, sharp monuments to our anxieties and insecurities – the folk sculpture of fear. They are often negative and limiting, so that the characteristics of their wisdom are the opposite of the gospel (the wisdom of men being the foolishness of God?).

The gospel is preached to remove insecurity, to give courage, to change fear into the limitless virtues of love and mercy. The proverb is very strong on keeping feet on the ground, and hands to the wheel, and noses to the grindstone – the gospel replies with a vision: Jesus raised his eyes to heaven and said: 'Father, the hour has come, glorify thy Son ...'

All through the gospels, Jesus has said, 'Fear not', and he has offered and promised peace. In today's gospel we see why he can say such things – we're like men with paper money being suddenly shown the treasury of gold which supports that paper. Thabor was a glimpse, but we didn't hear a word. Now we listen as the Second Person of the Trinity speaks to the First Person of the Trinity.

This is the prayer of God – strong and calm because it rests on omnipotence and total trust, personal in detail and address because it is spoken in love, and the language of love is never general.

We may listen cool and unmoved – just another inside story. The Apostles must have listened in wonder and wide-eyed. Was he talking about them to God, the Father? Did they feel proud or did they know what they were letting themselves in for? They would know in the years to come why he prayed for them and the power of his prayer. He had chosen the men for his mission and they were ready and he was handing over to them. 'I am not in the world any longer, but they are in the world and I am coming to you.'

If you want to see what the prayer of Christ did for them, look at the second reading. St Peter speaking. Echoes of Christ? Strength and calm and vision from a man who ran away and denied. Isn't he like the shy lad who goes to America for a couple of years and comes back confident and commanding? What would Simon's wife have made of this Peter? Was this the man she married? Transformed you might say.

Another proverb – listeners seldom hear good of themselves (so don't listen at doors). That's the wisdom of the human situation – but listen this time because Christ is speaking about us. 'I pray for them, for those you have given me, in them I am glorified.'

And here we are – the chosen people – with headaches, with land weighing down this man's soul, and money rustling in this man's mind, a girl's hair blowing through this boy's thoughts, and she wondering if the green jumper would go with the skirt, rheumatism creaking in her ladyship's knee, children crying at the back of your mind. We're here, perhaps not fully knowing why, half the time not wanting to be, and wishing we were somewhere else. We'd need God to change us – to transform us.

And so he prays for us – his latest set of men with a mission – the apostles for today, the seventh Sunday after Easter. All the Apostles were as unlikely as us – no personnel manager would have chosen them.

Pentecost Sunday

Sticks and stones, it is true, may break your bones, but it is not true that words may never hurt you. They will frequently, by design and by accident. And not just other people's – your own too.

We say things we don't mean, and things we don't mean to say. We say bitter destructive words because we are raw inside and our only satisfaction is to draw red claws through someone else's peace, too. We know we shouldn't say it, and we do. We all have a language problem.

It's deeper than we realise. If I say the word 'kitchen' you think you know what I mean. So it's a place you cook in – all right. On what? In my picture it's on a range. Does the window in your kitchen look out on a lake too? And the sewing machine is in the corner? Which corner? The one near the presses of course. Presses? We didn't have a dresser. A picture of Christ the King over the mantelpiece. And you have linoleum – we have tiles. Ours is cream, yours orange and brown, very nice. Kitchen? Are we talking about the same thing?

That's part of the trouble about talking to other people. They don't know the language. They can make the right sounds but they don't understand you. And you can't understand them. (Just think of all the parents who say that.)

In the end, I suppose, every person is another language and we have to learn each other's language – else we don't mean too much to one another. And that's what Christianity is about – understanding people, knowing the allowances you have to make for them – gift of understanding.

So the first miracle of the Christian Church – today's miracle – is the fulfilment in a little way of what Christianity is to do in all times and places. Christ's message and prayer is 'that they may be one', and its very first fulfilment was that people listened and understood. Barriers are broken down, borders disappear, and people are delighted – Egyptians and Libyans, Jews and Arabs. They share in the gift of understanding which is one of the gifts of the Holy Spirit. They are made one by him. We might, indeed, pray that he come again today to renew that part of the earth, and other nearer parts and peoples.

The Holy Spirit comes to give us words and meaning, to help us understand, to bring us closer, and to restore broken unity. He doesn't come to countries, he comes to people, to work wonders. Family therapists now say that most upset in homes is caused by misunderstanding. Father tells son to go out to the yard and bring him in a long piece of timber; son goes and brings in his idea of a long piece of timber, which happens to be three feet longer than father's idea. Father greets him, 'What kind of eejit …?' And at Mass the following Sunday they'll be saying: 'Did you hear about Michael – gone to England – had a row with the father?' We are, none of us, as transparent as we think – people can't read us like a book and we can't read other people. 'Sure, she must know I …' Must she? 'Sure, wouldn't any fool see …?' Would he? We all need to ask the Holy Spirit for the gift of understanding – so that we speak more clearly, listen more acutely.

You may be a very difficult language for other people. The Holy Spirit may simplify your tenses, make your moods a little less irregular, make you a little more indicative, a little less imperative.

For this is part of Pentecost, the Holy Spirit sent to bring us words that heal, and soothe and nourish and restore, words that bring new life. And he comes to live within us so that we will be like living sacraments whose very existence will be for others a soothing oil, nourishing bread, life-giving water.

The Feast of the Most Holy Trinity
There was a time when squared paper meant Fox and Geese, but it is no longer just the innocent battleground of noughts and crosses. Our lives now are plotted in the thin lines that run in peaks and shallows. The weather plunges down in a deep depression, the May trade figures show an upward swing, at the foot of the bed your temperature dances across the page.

If one had to graph the ordinary human life, there would, I suppose, be a fairly obvious pattern. The line of physical life would lead to a peak at about age twenty, stay on a plateau for a few years and then begin a descent. The descent would be gradual at first, and then fall steeply to a stop. The line of mental life would be much the same – stay on the plateau longer perhaps, descend and stop. The emotional lifeline would probably be more varied, some wild mountaintops and deep valleys, to mark first love, crushes, romances, despair, then settling to milder fluctuations, and again, and inevitably and finally a stop.

There would be only one line that would not stop, the line that leads out from baptism, the line that marked the life of God in us. It does not stop, it carries over the page and goes on forever.

Of course it's a very varied line. The way we're getting on with God is very different at different times. There would be parts of the page where the line would be running very thinly along the bottom, a very weak little line, while the other lines galloped strongly far above it. Then it might begin to rise slowly, perhaps as the others began to decline. It would rise as we realised that wealth and health wouldn't last forever, as we felt the need for God. It would begin to climb the page crossing the other lines that were on their way down. And what the graph would be saying is that many's the old man or woman – not as strong, not as bright as once they were – who is very close to God, and growing closer.

Baptism bides its time in us. The love that sent his only Son is a patient love. The life of God in us is a lifetime growth. Our baptism becomes fully operative in us at the moment of death. Its ceremonies are a symbol of Christ's death and Resurrection, and of our dying with him to rise with him. So it is at the moment of death that the life that was given with the pouring of water enters its own country and steps out in its newly minted glory.

We are baptised in the name of the Father and the Son and the Holy Spirit, and from that moment we live with their life and are under their protection. All the years we do things in their name, we bless ourselves and others in their name, we are confirmed, forgiven, anointed in their name. When life is over we go to meet them, to be with them forever.

The feast of the Trinity is the feast of the Holy Spirit who prays in us, of the Son who died for us, of the Father who loved the world so much. Celebrating the feast here on earth is like celebrating a birthday in a foreign land – a celebration that is some bit short of full happiness, that is not exactly in the right place. But there is still the exchange of love, our remembering of God and his remembering of us. We are assured again of his care for us, because he is, as Moses said, a God of tenderness and compassion, rich in kindness. One day we will meet him face-to-face and celebrate the feast of the Trinity at home. In the meantime the grace of the Lord Jesus Christ and the love of God and the fellowship of the Holy Spirit be with you all.

Corpus Christi

They say the Irish are not very good at giving public expression to their love. 'Public expression' – we generally think of people not kissing in front of their children and not finding it too easy to say 'Darling'. It is, I suppose, ironic and sad and understandable that the greatest public expression of love in any country is in the 'Deaths' page of its newspapers. 'Deeply regretted, profound sorrow, inexpressible grief, heartbroken' – the sad language with which love meets death; the stricken coinage of affection in which we all pay the price of love given and received.

They are brief words with whole histories behind them, lifelong friendships, laughing faces, a child that once brought joy, people standing round a grave.

Maybe that's a peculiarly Irish line of thought. Douglas Hyde wrote about it at the end of one of his books:

> The end! the end! The Gaels never forget it. *Respice finem*, 'Look to the end.' This is a word which used constantly to be in their mouths. Everything shall go by. Man's life shall go … Memory of him shall go … fame and name shall go, and at last, nobody shall know that we have ever been in it … They shall go, they shall all go, men and their glory, the writers and the books, the fame of those who have gone, the renown of those who shall come, there is only one thing, says the Connachtman, that shall be lasting in this world the grace of God.

The Religious Songs of Connacht – Douglas Hyde

Faced with our most ancient enemy, death, we seem to be beaten people – except – what did the Connachtman say?

No, we're not beaten. The quiet word of victory has been whispered to us, to every one of us, to you. 'Body of Christ. Amen. Body of Christ. Amen. Body of Christ. Amen.' And the priest has gone by, leaving us with the living bread and the promise of today's gospel: 'Anyone who eats this bread will live forever.'

Corpus Christi, Body of Christ – it's like a password which that grim sentry, death, must obey. By themselves our human loves and friendships, we at our most generous, must die. But Christ confers immortality on them and us. He makes all that is good in us stronger than death.

The promise is both personal and communal. The priest says 'Body of Christ' and it's a personal word from God saying 'I have promised you that you will live forever. I promise you again. Here I am as a sign.' It is the answer from God to an old Mayo prayer after Communion:

O Creator show me mercy
God of Heaven whose face is like the sun
Take the body that you visit
To yourself when all is done.

But at the altar look right and left, the line of people to whom the word has been given: Body of Christ; Body of Christ: Body of Christ … the promise made to you is made to others too. God says 'and you, and you, and you.'

Look right, look left – the future saints. That's the part we're in greater danger of forgetting, and it's what St Paul reminded us of this morning, 'that though there are many of us, we form a single body, for the bread we break is a communion with the body of Christ'.

So that small moment of communion when the priest says a hurried and maybe routine 'Body of Christ' and you answer 'Amen' if he gives you time, that's a moment to be treasured between you and God. A door opens for a brief instant on your future. God says, 'I have promised.' You say, 'Amen.' And what it means is that one day death will have no more dominion. The words on that page will all be changed – deeply regretted will be reunited, profound sorrow will be deepest happiness, inexpressible grief will be changed into joy so great that it has no words either – and the heartbroken will laugh together again.

Eighth Sunday of the Year
It may not be possible to serve God and Mammon, but how we try! We try not because we're bad people but because we're nervous people, and partly selfish, and afraid of the future.

We are afraid of the future because we know we are shortsighted and cannot see into it. So we worry about it, and about many things that are never going to happen. We plan for it and provide for it and insure against it. Some of our planning is prudent and some of it is purposeless – because it is planning for something that will never be.

But we don't know now which is prudent and which is not – so what do we do?

This morning's gospel says: 'Stop, take another look. Maybe you have got it all wrong. It's not the future you should worry about – it's your planning. That's what's causing the worry, that's what's destroying your peace. You can't see into the future at all but your main trouble is that you don't see the present very clearly either.'

We don't see God very clearly in the present. It isn't that we don't believe in Him, we're not really atheists – but you could call us functional atheists a lot of the time. He might as well not be there, most of the time for many of us. And it isn't that we have cut him deliberately out of our lives – more that he has dropped out, God the dropout.

For many of us he exists more as a guilty feeling than as a person – like people you should have written to and who come to haunt you for a moment at a bus stop or before you go to sleep. You'll send them a card at Christmas, or Easter, if you don't forget, if you have the time, if you get round to it.

For most of us, when God disappears off our map, it is not because we have rejected him or that we adore money or motorbikes in his place. It can be that, but most of us don't choose atheism, we lapse into it, and not from selfishness but from distraction. We are distracted people. And you'll pray to him tomorrow, if not today, if you don't forget, if you have the time, if you get round to it.

We are distracted, there are so many things – there's the car, a funny rattle in it, is it the thermostat they call it, you'll have to see about it, and the red light is on on the cooker again, and the oven won't come up and David has to have new shoes and there's another one for Confirmation and Carmel's First Communion, and you'd better see Mary before she leaves hospital or she'll never forgive you, and the ESB bill and look at the time it is, where's the tin opener – oh and that parent–teacher meeting, and 'The Brothers' are on tonight. Oh God! Oh who? What's his second name?

So we are in prison and the plans we have are the cells, and the things we have are our wardens. And Our Lord says this morning: 'I can set you free.' And you'll answer: 'But all these things have to be done.' And he says: 'Your heavenly Father knows you need them all, but don't set your heart on them like the pagans. Set your heart on God first and everything else will fall into place.'

And, if you're so afraid of the future that you must have a guarantee, listen again to this one, from God: 'Does a woman forget her baby at the breast, or fail to cherish the son of her womb? Yet even if these forget, I will never forget you.' I can never understand why the next line in the Bible isn't added to that, because it seems to me the ultimate guarantee – it is: 'See, I have branded you on the palms of my hands.' Every time you look at a crucifix you see a copy of that guarantee.

Homilies for June

Vol. 44, No. 5, May 1993

Trinity Sunday

The Trinity is a little like the telephone. It is difficult to explain how, with a few little numbers punched in, I can in seconds speak to someone on the other side of the world. It is difficult to explain but easy to do. And the explanation isn't the important thing. The important thing is its reality, its use, the communication it makes possible, the connections that are its meaning. The Trinity is a bit like that – difficult to explain but easy to know and the important thing is its reality, the communication it makes possible, the connections that are its meaning – the connections between me or you and the Father, and the Son and the Holy Spirit.

Today is the feast of the Trinity, of the Father, Son and Holy Spirit. God's feast they call it in some languages.

But what do you say when you preach about the Trinity? It's a mystery and it's difficult – so as we often say about hard things, 'Let us begin in the name of the Father and of the Son and of the Holy Spirit.' And that's to do it rightly, for we have bypassed the apparatus, we have made our call person-to-person and we have begun at the beginning – because before this world began there were from all eternity these three persons, the Father, the Son and the Holy Spirit. In the beginning and before the beginning was God.

St Patrick was right to begin there. The very first sermon preached in Ireland was on the Trinity according to our tradition, with the shamrock used to illustrate it according to our folklore. We began this Mass with 'In the name of the Father ...' so all our beginnings are in those names. The world began and we began because of the love of the Father, Son and Holy Spirit. Maybe we feel the Trinity hasn't much to do with everyday life, but the truth is, it has everything to do with everything, because nothing would exist without the Trinity. It's our beginning. They're our beginning.

They are also our end. They are home and we are on our way to them, on our way home. We sometimes talk about life as a journey, a pilgrimage, a long road, and a favourite Church image is that of a pilgrim people, always on the way. It's one picture of the Christian's life. But in the last few years, especially with the coming of more women theologians and writers, another picture has been painted to complement the journey, or perhaps to complete the identikit. This picture shows us the Christian's life as 'home'. And what's meant by 'home' is really the Trinity – love, hospitality, caring, welcome, people who refresh and renew you and mind you, people who send you out with a blessing, who pray for you while you're gone, and welcome you when you come back. That's what the Trinity is, God at home, the Three Persons living perfect love. Jesus comes to us from that home to bring us the Father's love and the Spirit's too. The Holy Spirit comes to us from that home to bring us the light of Christ, the inspiration of the Father. You see they're very close, like all the best families, and you'd know them out of each other.

This is their feast. It's God's feast. But it's ours too, because you see we're family now. We were made family in baptism, welcomed in, by the Father and the Son and the Holy Spirit, 'Who's this?' said God and our parents said, 'This is Elizabeth, this is Michael, this is Patrick,' and God said, 'Welcome in Elizabeth, welcome Michael, welcome Pat – make yourself at home.' We're all God's children, brought in to the light, the love, the warmth and the company of God, brought in home.

So we're celebrating our feast today as well as God's. That's what I'd say. I think God might simply say 'ours'. God would just include us because God would be much more aware of the full meaning of baptism. For God, we really are family. For us, we often forget.

Sometimes you see pictures in the papers of VIPs being welcomed or seen off on the tarmac at the door of a plane. I was never there myself, neither welcoming nor being welcomed. Like most people I'm at Gate 7A with one piece of hand luggage, a duty-free bag, and my boarding card in my hand or my teeth. We're not VIPs of the tarmac kind. But we're VIPs with God. Long ago they saw us off, Father, Son and Spirit – on the journey of life, and someday they'll be waiting to welcome us back home. In the meantime stay in touch. You don't do it by phone but by prayer. The prefix is three – in the name of the Father and the Son and the Holy Spirit.

Feast of Corpus Christi

'Death the Leveller' was the title of the poem and generations of pupils liked it and remember it. It was the first poem in the book. Maybe that helped. It had a good rhythm and rhyme, and its sentiments suited that strong sense of equality that fifteen-year-olds have.

> Sceptre and Crown
> Must tumble down,
> And in the dust be equal made
> With the poor crooked scythe and spade.

It's one of the persistent, pervading human thoughts, this levelling that death does. At last we're all equal. There are no pockets in a shroud, and you can't bribe God. We're equal before God, king and pauper, star, dullard.

It really oughtn't take death to teach that to a Christian. The Eucharist ought to do it at every Mass. When we stand in line to receive the Body of Christ we are pick 'n' mix, liquorice allsorts, rich poor, old young, tinker tailor. It's not that there's no favour. It's that everyone is favoured. Christ comes to us all as friend, as forgiveness for the past, as help for the present, as promise for the future. Christ is the leveller, but he levels differently from death. He levels not by reduction like death, but by raising us all up. And in our raising up he makes us a sign of the Resurrection of us all at the end. Why are we here this Thursday? To make us think of things like that and say thanks. Think and thanks – the special reasons for this feast of the Body of Christ. 'Take this all of you and eat it,' he said, 'This is my body.' And we do take it. Mass after Mass, Sunday after Sunday. We take it so often that we might take it for granted. So Corpus Christi is to make us stop and think – to stop us short in the middle of the week, in the middle of the year, to make us stop and think and thank.

The feast owes its origin to a woman, a Belgian woman, Juliana, who had a vision in the year 1209. She saw the moon, a full moon shining, but with a dark area on one side. The moon was the Church and the dark area represented how people were taking the Blessed Sacrament for granted. A feast was needed to remind us, and Juliana must have been a fairly persuasive woman because fifty-five years later Corpus Christi was a feast of the Universal Church. So we have this surprise feast to take the edge off routine and repetition, and make us think and thank.

What will we think about? Think about this – that God breaks bread with us, and we with God and with one another. And if we don't really break it with one another, do we really break it with God? Because we are gathered in here not as powerful and weak, not as smart and stupid, not as cool and culchie, but as God's people joined and cemented by Christ. We are gathered praying, 'May all of us who share in the Body and Blood of Christ be brought together in unity by the Holy Spirit.' All so that we can be the Body of Christ in the world, cementing and repairing the rifts and cracks of life. Think! We are to think about that.

And thank! – because that short moment of communion when the priest says 'Body of Christ' and you say 'Amen' is a moment to be treasured between you and God. For a brief instant a door opens on your future. 'Body of Christ' – it's like a password to a sentry – and it means 'You're one of Christ's people' and you say 'Amen', which means 'Indeed I know it.' It's the promise of eternal life given in every communion. 'He who eats this bread will live forever,' said Christ. To coin a phrase: Christ is the Word, and Christ is the man. The Eucharist is his promise that we will all sit down together with him around the table of God in heaven, sceptre, crown, scythe and spade, and there will never again be a dark side to the moon. Death will do no more levelling for death will be done. That's why we say thanks on this feast of the body and blood of Christ. Think and thank!

Eleventh Sunday of the Year

There's talk now of compassion fatigue. People see so much misery, hunger, war, disaster, cruelty, the long litany of human ills, that they switch off. We don't switch off the set, we switch off the mind, the heart, we feel hopeless and helpless. So we stop the world and get off.

Perhaps we need to go to the wizard, the Wizard of Oz – but equally, perhaps we don't want to go. For the three who accompanied Dorothy were the Scarecrow who wanted a mind, so that he could stop and think, and the Tin Man who wanted a heart, because without it he was just hollow, and the Lion who wanted courage so that he could be lion-hearted.

Perhaps we need to go to the wizard, and perhaps we don't want to go. Maybe we feel as the man says when he reluctantly gives the Tin Man a heart, 'Hearts are only practical when they're unbreakable.'

It would be a very practical world, a world of unbreakable hearts. It could be a very efficient, cost-effective world. Then taxes would be reduced considerably and government expenditure could be restricted to really essential services, like the road. In a world of unbreakable hearts the hungry would just die away and we would live with no uneasy nagging at our heartstrings or tugging at our purse strings. In a world of unbreakable hearts, we'd all be much better off, at least those of us who were healthy and wealthy, and there'd be no Trócaire or Gorta or Concern, and we'd be rid of the Red Cross, one less cross to carry. No Simons needed, and the Samaritan wouldn't have to stop, in a world of unbreakable hearts. Breakable hearts cost so much, oh the expense of them!

It would, of course, be a world without Christ. He wouldn't be needed in it, but neither could he live in it. It won't ever happen, but we do sometimes make attempts at creating it, politically or personally – when compassion drains out of the system, the state's or the citizen's. And when it does we are, in the most literal way, anti-Christ.

For Christ was for compassion. He was the compassionate Christ, the very incarnation of God's compassion for his people. Today's readings are the story of compassion from its beginnings in God, to its flowering in people. For the first reading is the heartfelt love and support of God for 'my very own', God's own not by domination but by love – 'I carried you on eagle's wings and brought you to myself.' And the Second Reading is the person-ification of God's love in Christ. God's love given mind and heart and courage in a human body that would die to prove its love. 'What proves that God loves us is that Christ died for us while we were still sinners.'

But before he died in compassion, he lived in compassion, for he saw the crowds and he felt sorry for them because they were harassed and dejected, like sheep without a shepherd. And because he was sorry for them he sent his disciples to them, to help and give new life and cleanse and cast out devils. He sent them with a heart and a half and they were to do it with a heart and a half.

Christ was God's compassion, the disciples were Christ's compassion. It's God telling us that compassion is a person. It's the little girl's cry to her mother at night, 'Stay with me, I'm lonely.' And the mother said, 'Oh, haven't you your dolls and your teddy?' and the little girl said, 'Ah, when you're lonely you need someone with skin on her face.'

The market for compassion has not lessened since Christ's time.

But who'll go? Why do you think God chose you to hear his word today? God does not work by accident. We are all to be the missionaries of his compassion. There are so many places, so many people who wait to be touched by Christ. There are so many unchristened places in all of us, so much desert in the human heart.

We have been sent to one another. This is the marvellous economy of God that we are to be one another's saviours, carrying Christ's healing with us wherever we go. And the harvest is rich and the labourers are always too few. Gentleness needs another voice – ours. Help needs another hand – ours. Compassion needs another touch: ours. Love needs feet to travel on – ours.

We know, Lord, you count on us and 'count us a kingdom of priests, a consecrated nation'. These are very big words and high ideals, Lord, for poor scarecrows without a mind, and empty tin men without a heart, and lions without courage. So we ask you, O Christ, our wizard, to give us your mind and your heart and your courage, so that your compassion may reach your people.

Twelfth Sunday of the Year
There was a man once who obviously hadn't read or listened to the three readings for this Sunday. He couldn't have – or he wouldn't have said:

God – must think it exceedingly odd
If he finds that this tree
Continues to be
When there's no one about in the quad.

He obviously thought God was not the be-all and the end-all of everything. I mean, he said, look at the tree! Standing there, leaves sprouting, branches waving, birds singing in it – and look! – no God! Rather like a little boy cycling with his hands off the handlebars –

'Look, no hands' – but you still need the bicycle or you can't cycle. You still need God or there's no tree. And whatever independence the tree has, or any one of us has, is still God-given, and God-sustained. Without God we wouldn't be, or be free. So thank God we exist. We exist, thank God.

Ah, but there are times, aren't there? There are times when we don't thank God for existing and don't feel a bit like thanking God. Oh it's not that we doubt God's existence. It's that we find our own a burden. We might have written the famous reply to the man who had his doubts.

> Dear Sir,
> Your astonishment's odd;
> I am always about in the quad.
> And that's why the tree
> Will continue to be
> Since observed by,
> Yours faithfully,
> God.

No, our question isn't about God's existence but about God's whereabouts. He's there all right, but where? So back to the three readings for this Sunday. They're answering questions we ask.

Where is God? When everything is against you and everyone's against you – where's God? The first reading says 'at your side, on your side'. In the middle of terror and error, when you're deafened by denunciation and the grimace of revenge – God is there with you. You have committed your cause to him and the Lord is at your side, 'a mighty hero'. You mustn't be afraid, says the first reading – since God is never away. And you will stand and not fall or fail, you who are God's – for even more than the tree you are always under the eyes of yours faithfully, God. Yours faithfully – even when we lose faith, or loyalty, God never does. God is ours, faithfully.

But, in the middle of sin and death, in a wicked and tragic world – where's God? What are God's promises worth, faced with sin and death? Is there forgiveness for the sin, mercy for the sinner, and can life defeat death? Can God come through on his promises? The second reading says, 'Oh yes, God will come through on his promises, certainly! And what's more, abundantly! And what's more still, freely! This God is not just faithful, but absolutely faithful! And this God is not a stingy God but generous beyond your dreams! And with this God – there's no charge!' And where's this God, this grace? The second reading answers: 'coming through the one man Jesus Christ'.

And so Jesus tells his friends in the gospel, tells them three times – Don't be afraid. He knew what those friends would face, the terrors, the denunciations, the revenge, the struggle with sin – their own and others; the fear of death – their own and others. Oh, he didn't need to be a prophet to know that – all he needed to be was human. But he needed to be God to tell them: Don't be afraid – I'm with you. God is with you always. Never mind the tree; even a sparrow in the tree or hopping on the ground is under God's eye and care always. Never mind the tree, never mind yourselves – and you're worth a lot of sparrows – aren't two of them sold for a penny (or five for tuppence says St Luke – like tickets in a raffle at a concert)? Oh you're worth a lot of sparrows. Why every hair on your head has been numbered. (I think he's smiling.) So there is no need to be afraid – you are worth more than hundreds of sparrows. (Oh, he's smiling definitely.) You are priceless. You are my friends and I never let my friends down. You are God's friends – God couldn't let you down. So don't be afraid. That's the bottom line – yours faithfully, God.

Thirteenth Sunday of the Year

'WANTED! REWARD!' Imagine one of these police posters. The word 'WANTED' on top, then a photograph underneath, then the word 'REWARD'. And the person in the photograph is you. You're wanted and there's a reward.

There's a story about a man coming out of a church saying, 'That was the loveliest sermon I ever heard. The priest didn't mention me once.' That won't happen this evening, and if you had any ideas it might, let me do what Christ did and throw cold water on the idea. We're all in this evening's gospel – the gospel of the cup of cold water, we're all 'wanted', and the mugshot is yours.

But we're not in the gospel to be frightened or blamed or accused. There's no threat, only a promise.

We have been given – every single one of us – a gift, and we can use this gift well or badly. The gift is power over one another. We get it the moment we're born – perhaps earlier. We have it until our last breath – perhaps later. Even a baby with a smile can set a whole house smiling, with a cry can wake, upset, set a whole house running. But a little older it becomes a power of life or death. We can kill with a look. With one word, a reputation, a hope, a friendship dies. A smile can be forgiveness and the beginning of a new world, one word can bring new life. Someone's treachery can murder you, someone's kindness can bring you back from the dead, a resurrection.

Don't think of the times you have done this, think first of the times it was done to you. You get a better picture with a good negative – when you remember how you felt, the blush of shame when someone hurt you, the flush of pride when someone praised you. We remember these. We often forget the power we have that can cause them in others.

That's why I think it was a hot day and Our Lord was thirsty when he said 'Even a cup of water will get its reward.' Maybe he thought too of the day he'd be desperate on the cross, saying 'I thirst', and he'd have loved a cup of cold water.

It's that cup of cold water that has us at Mass, that makes us say, 'Let us pray', and not, 'Let me pray', that makes us say, 'Lord graciously hear us', not 'Lord, graciously hear me.' If you're thirsty and I have the water, then my cup of cold water to you is the way I give you God, the way God graciously hears both of us.

The whole point of prayer is that it should make us aware of other people. You can't run a limited company with only yourself and God as shareholders. Anyway, God does not hold with limited companies. Limited companies are part of the business of this world, not of the next. God refuses to be exclusive.

You remember going to school – learning that there were three persons not just in God, but in grammar, first, second, third, I, You, He or She. Well, to leave out the second and third persons would not only be poor grammar, but poor religion too. Our prayers would be like the Tarzan films when Tarzan knew only two words 'Me Tarzan'. If Tarzan is to pray he must also learn 'You Jane' and see Jack and Jill too.

God will not play in a restricted script, a 'me' script or a 'just you and me' script. God, true to God, insists that the three persons are part of any real prayer. Indeed, not just part of it but the point of it. 'Anyone who welcomes you welcomes me, and welcomes the one who sent me,' says Christ.

And Christ comes in all sorts of shapes and sizes. The hero has a thousand faces. But however he comes and whatever face he wears he will give eternal thanks for hospitality – hospitality of word, hospitality of deed, hospitality of thought. Our badness he will forgive but our goodness he will never forget. Even a cup of cold water, he said, I will never forget it for you.

So you think back to that poster – WANTED. You know who's wanted. And REWARD – you know it's guaranteed. And you know whose picture lies between wanted and reward. You recognise yourself? It wasn't I put your picture there. It was Christ who put it there on the day you were baptised. You're the one he wants. And he has high hopes for you, high hopes that you'll be nice to him when you meet him.

Homilies for July

Vol. 37, No. 6, June 1986

Fourteenth Sunday of the Year

Isn't it nice to see so many people happy? Oh, don't look round. I'm talking about the gospel. There are seventy-three delighted people, Jesus and the seventy-two he sent ahead of him, bearing gifts of peace and healing and good news. They're back now and they are delighted.

Our Lord sent them out calmly with very sober instructions. They're back and they are not calm. They are rejoicing. 'Lord,' they said, 'even the devils submit to us when we use your name.'

And Our Lord is pleased as Punch. Have you ever watched a father or mother on a sideline or at a wedding, proud and happy about their child? These disciples are bubbling round him and he's happy with them and for them.

Then he does two things that are the sort of things that parents do. He becomes reflective and he begins to look into the future. He sees a little bit farther than the children and he tries to give more meaning to what they have done and to make them see farther too.

Like the proud parent who has visions of all-Ireland finals and Internationals and the Olympics in 1996, Jesus sees the kind of future these disciples could have, the sort of work they could do. 'I have watched Satan', he said, 'fall like lightning from heaven.' He senses the power of his disciples. If they stayed as good as they were, as enthusiastic, as generous, then there was no limit to the good they would do.

There was evil in the world then as now, the evil of evil minds and hearts, the evil of pain, the evil of anxiety, the evil of poverty. But Jesus saw suddenly in his friends as he looked at them, the way to change the world. He saw, as he watched them, how evil could be beaten, how the bad could be changed into good. He sees Satan fall, but not through condemnation or blaming, not through wishful thinking or saying 'Isn't it awful?' not through any of these things but through people, ordinary people.

It isn't often Our Lord acts triumphant but he does here. And what's extraordinary is that it's the triumph of the ordinary. He's rejoicing in the possibilities of ordinary people. Once you have seventy-two people on any sort of committee you are talking of ordinary – not handpicked, not special, not high fliers. He's delighted with his people. This is power to the people – the power of God, in the people of God. This is Jesus with his people saying 'We shall overcome.' He sees his work and his hopes in good hands. They have gone out like copies of himself and they have done good to all they met.

Mission accomplished. Was it mission impossible? Is that mission impossible now? Could we do it now? I said to you at the beginning 'don't look round'. Look around now. Could we be today's seventy-two? If Jesus stood among us this minute and said, 'I want people – seventy-two will do, but I'll take as many as I get' – would you volunteer? If he said,

> I want you to go out and make peace in your homes. I want you to help the depressed, to pity the suffering, understand the pain, forgive the foolish, give another chance to the beaten. I want you to get rid of the devils of greed, and selfishness, and bossiness and dishonesty, and jealousy.

If he suddenly stood here and said that – would you volunteer? And if he said, 'And I'm with you all the way' – would it help? Would you volunteer and would it be mission impossible, if he were here?

I said 'if he were here'. Don't look around. I think he is here. He's asking, and he's not looking for answers. He's looking for people. We're the only answer.

I read last year of an American doctor, Dr Behrhorst, who worked in a South American Indian village for twenty-two years. When he went there they were diseased and starving. Slowly with his help they began to improve in health, in hope, in work. An old Indian woman spoke to a reporter about the doctor. 'He saved us,' she said. 'We wish he was a piece of paper so that we could make many copies of him. If there were a machine for copying people we could make thousands of copies of the doctor and then we could save the world.' That's what she said. Well there's no such machine – but there are a lot of us here.

Only don't be vague or leave it until tomorrow. You're needed at home, today.

Fifteenth Sunday of the Year
Someone once said that all the important questions in life are short – Who are you? What's your name? Do you love me? Will you marry me? What is it, doctor? Why? How long? How far? When? You can make your own list, but don't forget to add today's short question, 'Who is my neighbour?'

It was the question the lawyer put to Jesus. He asked it almost triumphantly, as if he were in the district court in Galilee. The witness had just said, 'You must love God and love your neighbour.' Then the lawyer pounced. 'And who is my neighbour?' he said, stabbing out his finger and fixing the prophet from Nazareth with his eye.

The prophet looked coolly back. 'Not giving you a short answer.' He said, 'there was a man went down from Jerusalem to Jericho …'; it wasn't a short answer. It was the story of the Good Samaritan.

It's not a far-away and long-ago story. It's a today story. It will happen a million times on a million roads today. And it's not an other-people story; it's a me-and-you story. It's a little drama that will be played out on many stages this day.

And when the names go up at the end of the play, what part will you and I have played? 'The part of the Good Samaritan was played by … the passers-by were played by … the part of the wounded man was played by …'

I look at you and you look at me and we both see all the actors. For in this story one person is generous and kind and courageous and sometimes you are like that and I'm like that. The passers-by are indifferent or afraid or too carefully minding their own business – and we recognise our brothers, the family resemblance is striking, how like them we are. Sometimes we too won't stop, we're blind because we don't want to see, we're deaf because we don't want to hear. And sometimes we are the wounded man, helpless, unable to ask, afraid to ask. From the ground we watch the feet pass by; nobody seems to care. But we know how much it means when finally one pair of feet stop – we matter to somebody and immediately our wounds begin to heal.

So the story turns out to be our story. This is Your Life. Can you imagine it? For yourself? I don't mean the Eamonn Andrews kind exactly, where everybody remembers only the nicest things. Imagine it, someone coming in who says, 'Oh yes I remember you well – will I ever forget? – you didn't see me, it didn't suit you, but I saw you and I needed you and you passed by.' This is Your Life … Or your wife or your husband coming in perhaps, and instead of remembering great things saying, 'I know you didn't mean it but you never noticed me the day I …'

This is Your Life. Oh, there would be good things too when anyone would mistake you for the Good Samaritan – when you did notice and care and stop, and your time and your money and above all your love to heal someone near and dear or someone far away and hungry in Ethiopia.

The road from Jerusalem to Jericho is a very strange road. We're all on it and it's not out in Palestine at all. It runs by our own windows, through our own houses, through our very hearts.

One other short question: Which part do you feel best after playing – the passer-by or the one who stopped? There's no doubt which costs more but there's no doubt either which raises us up with the force of a resurrection and which casts us down with the force of a damnation.

Well, who is my neighbour? The question remains. God help us give the right answer and not tomorrow and not far away but in our own place today. So when the programme is over and the book is closed and handed to us with the words 'This is Your Life' that we may be glad and not ashamed to take it in our hands, and not afraid to open it.

A modern poet sums it up well in a poem called 'The Jericho Road':

A man went up on the Jericho road
He went up all alone
He was beaten up and left for dead
And all his money had gone.

and the Chorus goes:

Who is neighbour to this fellow?
Who'll stop to share his load?

Who gives a damn for the nameless man
On the other side of the road?

The Jericho road runs through our world
From Cape Town to Notting Hill,
And the Christ who told of the nameless man
Is asking his question still.

Who is neighbour to this fellow?
Who'll stop and share his load?
Who gives a damn for the nameless man
On the other side of the road?

'Jericho Road', Vincent Lyon

Sixteenth Sunday of the Year

An interesting story and it makes me uncomfortable. It seems unfair. I wish I knew what Mary and Jesus were talking about.

Poor Martha, I feel so much on her side and if I asked this minute, 'Hands up all who are for Martha.' I'd say most of you would vote like me for her.

My picture of her is wearing an apron and her face hot from being over the fire cooking. She's wiping her hands on the apron and then as she says, 'Lord, do you not care ...', she pushes back a stray strand of hair from her face. And Mary looks cool and peaceful and manicured.

Martha is there at the door and we know that a minute before she had been out in the kitchen saying, 'Where's that Mary? Wouldn't you think she'd ...'

We sympathise with her, and so does Our Lord – but he doesn't say she's right. He doesn't say, 'Mary will be out in a minute' or 'Go out and help your sister' or 'Amn't I terrible keeping her in here like this and you with so much to do outside?' He says none of these things, and we might have said any or all of them.

And it's not that he's against work, or hospitality, or against people helping people – I mean 'Love your neighbour' sums up all his teaching. Yet in this little family squabble he rules against Martha. Are we for her because we are like her?

So where are we? I'm for Martha and you're for Martha, and he's for Mary. Are we missing something, missing something as Martha was? Are we for her because we are like her? Because we can see with her eyes, see what she sees but can't see what he sees? Have we perfect sight and defective vision?

Christ takes Mary's part and he forces us to look again and this time question our judgement, not his. We are standing there in the door with Martha and he's saying, 'Stop and think and look for the meaning of your life. For once don't just do something, sit there.'

He's talking to people whose lives are like Martha's, full of worry and fret about many things. You have your own list of wild animals that are pulling you to pieces and destroying your peace – money, job, people, house, car, doctor, dancing lessons, holidays, wedding invitation, wallpaper, weeds. We haven't a minute. We're like the man who got up on his horse and galloped off madly in all directions at once. Or like the other man on the galloping horse who, when asked where he was going, shouted, 'I don't know, ask the horse.'

For many of us life is a galloping horse and we don't have or want time to think. 'Martha, Martha,' he says, 'you worry and fret about so many things, and yet few are needed. Indeed only one.'

I think Our Lord is saying that we can be too busy, too concerned about too many things – quantity destroying quality. No wasted time but a lot of wasted spirit. We can think there is value only in what has a price – what you can count like money, or put a price on, like a house or a hi-fi. And if we are concerned only about what is priced, then we can miss what is priceless.

I think that's what he was saying when he said Mary had chosen the better part. I think we sometimes say it ourselves. Did you ever find yourself saying or noticing or thinking or complaining that we don't give one another enough talk or enough attention – did you ever think it about parents and children maybe, husbands and wives, friends, people in hospital – plenty of things but not enough time or talk? We sometimes miss the better part.

So what were Mary and Our Lord talking about? Sometimes you get light, like the Wise Men, from unexpected stars. In the musical, *Man of La Mancha*, the Duke says to Cervantes, the great writer, 'A man must come to terms with life as it is.' The writer replies:

> I have lived nearly fifty years and I have seen life as it is. Pain, misery, hunger … cruelty. I have held men in my arms at the final

moment. They were men who saw life as it is, yet they died despairing. No glory, no gallant last words, only their eyes filled with confusion whimpering the question: Why?

I do not think they were asking why they were dying but why they had lived.

When life itself seems lunatic who knows where madness lies? Perhaps to be too practical is madness. To surrender dreams – this may be madness. To seek treasure where there is only trash. Too much sanity may be madness. And maddest of all, to see life as it is and not as it should be.

That's what the great writer said. Martha was seeing life as it is and, I think, Christ and her sister were talking about life as it should be.

Seventeenth Sunday of the Year

I suppose the first three words most human beings learn and attempt to say are 'Dadda' and 'Mamma' and 'gimme'. They're three extraordinary words, they're half our history, half our life story. 'Dadda' and 'Mamma' are the first words of first love and deep relationship – our lives are shaped by the way they love us and the way we love them. 'Gimme' is the word of need – our need for whatever we feel like as a child and at times it is the complete expression of our being, for sometimes even as adults we are just a bundle of needs. And of course it goes on all our lives – gimme a light, gimme a minute, gimme a break. We say 'gimme' to the boss and 'gimme' to the government.

Does it remind you of the way we pray – of what Our Lord is talking about today? He knew us and the kind of us: he was one of us – he came up the hard way like us all – baby, child, little boy, adolescent, young man. So he meets us where we are and when the disciples said 'teach us to pray', he taught them 'Our Father, give us this day our daily bread' – which is really an adult form of 'Dadda gimme'. And our Christian prayers are so often prayers to Mary Our Mother for what we need and to God our Father for what we need.

Sometimes people feel ashamed about their prayers. We say 'The only time I pray is when I want something. I'm always saying "gimme".' But maybe today would change your mind for today is the day 'gimme' is given respectability by God. Our Lord didn't despise 'gimme'. On the contrary, he says, 'Say it and say it again and again.'

He said once we should be like little children – maybe he was thinking of prayer. As any parent here knows even the smallest children will say gimme and gimme and gimme again, until they wear away the stone of your 'No! leave me alone, I said no! Go out and play, not now – Oh well, all right.' You give in to gimme. You know when you're beaten. Their persistence lasts longer than your opposition or your patience.

What is Christ saying today – about that man who wakes up the house looking for the three loaves? The man inside shouts 'Go away! We're all in bed.' But, says Christ, if he asks long enough, he'll get it. Friendship may not do it for him, but persistence will.

So Christ says, 'Ask and it will be given to you, search and you will find, knock and the door will be opened.' For, he says, the one who asks always receives, the one who searches always finds, the one who knocks will have the door opened.

Now that's an extraordinary statement – not only does Our Lord tell us to ask but he guarantees an answer. He doesn't say 'immediately' but he does say 'always'. He doesn't say that it will be exactly what you looked for – because as you and I know, children and fairly short-sighted adults don't always know what they're asking for. What he does say is, 'As sure as God is good you'll get the best thing there is.' That's the guarantee, 'as sure as God is good'. He says if a good father on earth would give only good things to his child – what do you think God our Father in heaven will do?

So don't be afraid to say 'gimme'. You began to say it in your family and when you're talking to God you're still saying it at home. And it's a way of sharing your needs with him – it's an invitation to God to be part of what you care most deeply about, whether it's a sick child, or somebody in pain or trouble or looking for a job. If it matters to you it matters to him.

Only the one thing Our Lord seems to say are useless are pale prayers; when it doesn't matter much to you, then there are no answers. The half-hearted prayer opens no doors. Sometimes I think of this when we say the Prayers of the Faithful or even the prayers of the Mass. There isn't enough of us in them. 'Lord graciously hear us' we say – and he'd want to have a sharp ear to hear because our voices are there but our hearts aren't in it. And that's what Our Lord is saying in today's gospel. He tells us what the content should be, what we should pray for – and then he tells us about the quality, the way we should pray – wanting, asking, hammering on the doors of heaven. St Ambrose assured St Monica – who was worried about her wild son Augustine – that he couldn't be lost. 'How do you know?' she said. 'Because', he said, 'the child of tears like yours couldn't be lost.' That's what's sometimes wrong with our prayers – there's no blood or sweat or tears in them. A pale gimme gets you nothing and no prayer takes hold of God that does not first take hold of man.

So Lord, teach us to pray,
Lord, hear us.
Lord, graciously hear us.

Homilies for October

Vol. 22, No. 9, September 1971

Twenty-Seventh Sunday of the Year

On long journeys airlines are very concerned that their passengers should not feel the time passing. With music, films, food, they try to make hours fly faster. They are almost apologetic that the transport should last so long and if there should be a delay of an hour or two we all accept there is reason for complaint and apology.

When those long-distance journeys took as many weeks as they now take hours nobody was entertained, nobody complained, nobody apologised. However, we now have a world where so many things are instant – coffee, answers, communications, death – that we have grown to expect the instantaneous and anything less (or is it more?) is an affront to our technology and our being. It is, perhaps, all part of our advance to that point where men shall be as gods, no longer confined by the restrictions of space and time – where we shall live in an eternal 'inst.' with no 'ult.' and no 'prox.' But we may lose something along the way – like patience.

Children do not have very much patience and as we come closer to the God-like position of having our wishes granted instantly we may revert to the child-like position of upset, dismay, helplessness and anger when they are not granted instantly.

When we pray for something and there is no answer or the answer seems to be 'No', we can lose faith in prayer, if not in God; we can lose hope, feel helpless, be angry. We may complain like today's reading 'How long ...?' 'Why ...?' and our case is so reasonable – surely God, like us, is against tyranny, outrage, violence and discord?

But God may be using our prayer of petition in another way, as a means of instruction and growth. In refusing to answer instantly he may be treating us as adults, weaning us from the child's 'Give me' and forcing on us the grown-up prerogative of doing things for ourselves.

Education is a new way of seeing things and the result of our prayers of petition is often not a solution but a vision. We begin to see that our personal world is a problem set for our personal solution. In learning to wait and to work towards that solution we grow in wisdom and in grace. Long before the term was thought of, God was a non-directive counsellor, educating us to find the answer, not handing us a ready-made one. The vision for our time is that the reshaping of our world, personal, social, political, is ours – but ours as architects and builders, not slave labour. The promise is 'if it comes slowly, wait – for come it will without fail.'

Twenty-Eighth Sunday of the Year
Today's reading gave the world one of its most famous and representative groups of people – 'the other nine'. We have all been among them at one time or other.

They are off-stage in the final act but we can imagine their happiness – to be back with wife and children again, to look into a mirror again and like what looked back, to be rid of bandages, wear a clean shirt, to need two shoes again, to walk down a street and greet and be greeted, to be back in business. Maybe they wondered where the tenth man was and explained by saying he was a foreigner. Foreigners are funny – but we can learn from them.

Ingratitude is usually forgetfulness and gratitude is remembrance. Our Eucharist is 'in memory of me'. 'In memory of his death and resurrection.' We fail to be grateful because we forget others too easily and remember ourselves too well. So parents keep reminding their children to 'say thanks'. It's not only children who need to be reminded.

Sometimes, of course, we are uncomfortable with the idea that we ought to be grateful. We can resent its implication – its suggestion of inferiority. The gift we give as a sign of gratitude may be simply our release from the burden of feeling grateful.

Gratitude is a burden because it imposes something on us. Like grace it should bring us to share with others the God and the good we receive. At its most complete it is an act of praise of God and an inspiration to greater generosity. The magnificent and the universal motherhood belongs to Mary who was full of grace. Today's reading is probably the best gospel foundation for Belloc's 'The grace of God is in courtesy' – that courtesy which is a restraint of one's devotion to oneself and an awareness of others. It is the quality we and Christ miss in the other nine!

Twenty-Ninth Sunday of the Year
In idiom and character the story of the widow and the unjust judge reads like Damon Runyon two thousand years before his time. It has his repetition of phrase and the oddly dignified dialogue he gave his villains.

'There was a judge in a certain town, who had neither fear of God nor respect for man. In the same town there was a widow who kept on coming to him and saying, "I want justice from you against my enemy." For a long time he refused but at last he said to himself, "Maybe I have neither fear of God nor respect for man but since she keeps pestering me I must give this widow her just rights or she will persist in coming and worry me to death."'

That certain town can't but might have been New York. The widow we can see – thin, small, fearless, black-robed, black-hatted, shaking her umbrella at the heavy expansive gangster boss with his cigar, his fedora, his bow tie, his bootleg Scotch. He knows his reputation and rejoices in it, and we can see him flick the ash as he turns to his henchmen and says that marvellous 'Maybe …'.

The idiom is twentieth-century, the moral is present-day – 'the need to pray continually and never lose heart'. Many Christians today are losing heart, perhaps because they don't pray enough. There is a lot of discouragement and hopelessness. Dedication to work or belief has been devalued by materialism and a rather crude acceptance of man's ultimate selfishness – 'Everyone is in it for what he can get out of it.' Earnestness, unless it is on one's own behalf, has become one of the stock comic qualities, and enthusiasm is suspect as being either false or unreasonable. In this sort of climate it is more difficult than ever for the Christian not to lose heart.

What makes it more difficult still is that we communicate discouragement to one another. The grudging service of the doctor or waitress or shop assistant or official or priest leaves only grudges in its wake. We come to expect poor service and to give poor service. We come to expect that promises will be empty and that hopes will be dashed. So we are the beaten people and it is only reasonable ('and statistics prove it') to expect failure, to expect that the world cannot be changed.

But it was the reasonable people who said Columbus would fall off the edge. And it is Christ who says today that his promises are not empty and don't lose heart. We can communicate courage as easily as despair and if we are dedicated in our work and life we influence others to do their work well.

To point his lesson Christ pits the stereotype of weakness, the widow, against power at its most ruthless. She won because she did not lose heart. We are to pray continually, to remain in contact with Christ the source of strength so that we do not lose heart. Then we shall overcome.

Thirtieth Sunday of the Year
This is the gospel of odious comparisons. With any story that has become proverbial there is the possibility that our appreciation remains at the level of our childhood memories of it. This one so easily fits the patterns we grew up with – the good guy and the bad guy – that we often fail to see its reality for us now.

Boasting is one of the first moral excesses a child notices and dislikes. So from the beginning we easily disliked the boasting Pharisee and readily identified with the poor publican. In doing so our reaction could be unconsciously Pharisaical – 'I wouldn't boast like that, I wouldn't look down on people like that, I wouldn't say such a thing about the publican.' When one thinks of it like that one can wonder if there isn't a third person in the story, standing very close to the Pharisee – oneself.

In the parable the hero and the villain are clearly identified for us. It is not always as easy to be sure in real life. Some of us boast very cleverly and some of us still make comparisons but are wise enough not to breathe a word to anyone about it. So surrounded as we are by clever and wise, the best thing is not to set ourselves up as judges because we are not the best judges. We do not always know fully even our own motivations and we are likely to be wrong in assessing the motivations of others. Only God can measure the real worth of any human being – that unique product of heredity, environment, opportunities, failures.

Neither must we demand that everyone else lives to our specifications. There are different ways of being good. Those who feel virtuous are wrong to demand that there shall be no more cakes and ale. If, for instance, we are always up and doing at 7 a.m. we should not be annoyed or offended by those who stir an hour later. Why such annoyance? Is there a trace of it in the Pharisee? As we read the story again and get past our childhood identifications perhaps we find a little bit more of the Pharisee in us and a little bit less of the publican than we first imagined. *Hypocrite lecteur, mon semblable, mon frère* ('Hypocrite lecturer, my likeness, my brother'; *Les Fleurs du Mal*, Charles Baudelaire).

Thirty-First Sunday of the Year

The reading from the Book of Wisdom swings us through the universe and lets us see the Earth through the eyes of God. We begin far out in space. Our Earth is 'like a grain of dust', a tiny star in the sky of some other planet, shining 'like a drop of morning dew'.

Then we come closer and see Earth, which might have been just another barren star, given life, made a home for plants and animals and human beings, through the love of God. Everything in it – especially its people – is mantled in his love. 'Yes, you love all that exists. You spare all things because all things are yours, Lord, lover of life, you whose imperishable Spirit is in all.'

We do not often think of God's mercy and love extending to things, or that our attitudes to them and use of them should reflect his respect for all that he has made. If we could always see our Earth as God sees it there would probably be no need for anti-pollution laws or conservation policies. Our dream world would exist – pure air, pure water, fruitful soil, unspoiled country, happy people. But so far are we from it that American weather reports now state whether the air is 'acceptable' and we have commissions and laws to protect natural beauty and wildlife from man the predator. We tend to be short-sighted, to take the short-term views and the sad results of our myopia are daily charted by ecologists.

And so scientists, oddly enough, are now asking us to save the world. They are speaking of the physical world, of course, but strangely what they ask is part of our Christian task too. What God created and loves has been given into our stewardship so that we may preserve and enjoy it, not destroy. Even more strangely, the means of redemption of the physical world are those of our own salvation. Redemption, for things and people, comes through our care and concern. So closely does our natural world parallel the supernatural.

It should not surprise us. St Paul thinks of all created things sharing in Christ's redemption and the love St Francis had for things was not an accidental part of his sanctity. This reading tells us how we should treat all God's creatures – not with adoration, not with contempt, but with respect and love. That is the way God looks at things.

'It is right to give him thanks and praise'

Vol. 21, No. 12, December 1990

I don't know about you, but I don't exactly love travelling in aeroplanes. I'm always happy, as the man said, to have ground under me and my feet on it. But I do love films about aeroplanes, and I love those countdown procedures that sound so efficient and scientific, as the captain and his co-pilots check everything before take-off.

You know the kind of thing: 'Ignition,' says the captain; 'Ignition,' says the co-pilot. 'Flaps,' says the captain; 'Flaps,' says the co-pilot. 'Doors to automatic'; 'Doors to automatic' – and the great machine begins to roll.

You see it too when fellows are pushing a car: 'Let off the brake'; 'Right.' 'Put her in gear'; 'Right.' 'Let in the clutch'; 'Right?' 'Right' – and the push begins, and in a few seconds the engine coughs into life and the car is off in a puff of blue smoke.

Now something very like that happens in the Mass, at the preface. The readings are over, sermon done, the gifts brought up, bread offered, chalice offered, hands washed, a little get ready prayer, everything 'in order, prayer over – and then the solemn central part of the Mass begins with a dialogue between priest and people – captain to co-pilots.

> The Lord be with you, says the priest.
> And also with you, say the people.
> Lift up you hearts, Check.
> We lift them up to the Lord, Right.
> Let us give thanks to the Lord our God, Right?
> It is right to give him thanks and praise, Right, Right.

And the Mass moves into the Eucharist. A new power takes over. Suddenly people and priest take on a new meaning. We begin to leave the earth. We reach for God.

There's bread – but in a few moments it will no longer be bread. There's wine – but in a few moments it will no longer be wine.

Bread and wine are about to make the strangest journey things ever made – from the inanimate, inert things they are, to become the Body and Blood of Christ, God and man.

And we, as our hearts are lifted up, become raised up ourselves. We're no longer ordinary people with our feet on the solid ground, stuck in the mud of Monday. The earth gives way, heaven opens, and we join the angels and saints as they sing their unending hymn of praise: Holy, Holy, Holy Lord, God of power and might.

With the angels and saints! Us? Who are we? Where are we? And we begin to talk directly to the Father: 'Father, you are holy indeed.' And we enter into the mystery of the Trinity, as part of their work: 'All life comes from you through your son Jesus Christ, by the working of the Holy Spirit.'

Who are we now? We're everybody, from all times and places, the gathered people of everywhere giving glory to God, calling on the Father, by the power of the Holy Spirit to make holy this bread and wine so that they may become the Body and Blood of Christ.

Can this really be us? Standing before the Father, like Moses, like Abraham, like Elijah, striking the rock, setting the altar, calling for the lightning – breaking out of time and place, demanding that God break in. Let the Supper Room be, let Calvary be, let the world's best gift of Christ to God be given. Priest speaks: This is my Body, This is my Blood.

And then we proclaim the mystery of faith. If we really could appreciate what was happening, we would probably proclaim it with a shiver and in a whisper, or we mightn't be able to talk at all. We have wrestled with angels, we have climbed the mountain of God, we have clamoured for a saviour, and God has given us Christ. It is right that in a tremendous silence the host be lifted up, the bell be rung, and our eyes raised and our heads bowed. For we have knocked at heaven's gate and God has opened at our knocking. And who are we? Whoever we are it is right to give him thanks and praise.

But who are we? Well, we're strange people, extraordinary people. Now, you might agree that we're strange people in the way the famous Quaker proverb says it: 'All the world's a little strange, friend, except me and thee – and even thee, friend, art a little strange.' I once heard an American translate that into modern

English: 'Everybody's crazy except me and you, and you're not so sure about me.'

Now, I don't mean strange that way and I do mean we are extraordinary people. But you'll look round and say: 'Look at us: we've dragged ourselves in, some with worries, some with woes from a world that's working, warring, weeping – we're only little people whose decisions don't shake the earth; whose decisions, when we can make decisions, don't even change ourselves. We're people here looking for help' – and here am I saying you're extraordinary, so you're not so sure about me.

Well, let me take you on two journeys. Come fly with me. Right? Right.

On the first journey we'll travel back in time. We'll make a stop a little way back, and then we'll fly over the centuries and the next stop will be the year 200 in Rome. The first stop is a special little stop for everyone. It might be fifteen years back for you or fifty or ninety – it's the day you were baptised, the day God welcomed you into his family, welcomed you to be like him, a creator, a redeemer, an inspirer; the day God marked you as someone who would know time as temporary, and the solid earth as insubstantial, for time and earth would be for you only preludes to the eternal and the infinite. You were given power to move between time and eternity, between the created universe and the uncreated God – not merely given power, but given mission: the mission to be priest to the finite and the infinite. For by baptism we are to be bridges along which will cross and run the prayers of the people to God and the mercy of God to his people. By baptism too, each of us is ordained to be a meeting place of love, a trysting place for the love of God and man and woman.

Oh, you may indeed have rheumatism in your fingers, or a light purse or a heavy heart, but on that day we're stopped at – twenty or forty or sixty years ago – the day you were baptised you stopped being ordinary.

But let's move on or we'll be here all day. We go back through the centuries over the first smoke of factories, over people in famine, people in plague, people at Mass rocks, people working in fields, monks, nuns – and as we travel we pick up year after year, century after century, the voices of people like us, who gathered themselves as we do today, to recreate Calvary, to have Christ feed the hungry again, to have his blood stream in the firmament again – voices that proclaimed the mystery of faith like us and like us said, 'It is right to give him thanks and praise.' Back we go to Rome in the year 200 and in the catacombs the voices are saying, 'It is right to give him thanks and praise.' And fifty years earlier St Justin at Rome tells us, 'The President of our Assembly takes the bread and chalice with wine and water and continues with a prayer of thanksgiving – the Eucharist.'

And ninety years earlier still at the end of the first century, the voices rise to say, 'O, Father, we thank thee, we thank thee.' And our last stop is in Jerusalem seventy years before, the Upper Room, a Thursday night, the night before the first Good Friday and the voice we hear is the voice of Christ – he took bread and when he had given thanks he broke it and gave it to them saying, 'This is my Body.'

From that first voice to the very latest voices, from him to us, the word is thanks, but then that's what the word Eucharist means – thanks.

'It is right to give him thanks and praise,' we say, and we know who began it and where it began. We know it is the gathered voice of the world echoing the voice of Christ, 'from age to age you gather a people to yourself so that from east to west a perfect offering may be made to the glory of your name'. It is, perhaps, even more right to gather at Knock from East and West and to give him thanks, because Knock began 111 years ago tomorrow night with a eucharistic cry from the lips of Brigid Trench, *'Cead míle buíochas do Dhia'* – one hundred thousand thanks to God. This place is full of echoes.

So we say, 'It is right to give him thanks and praise' and we know where it began and who began it. We don't always realise where it will end, and that it will never end.

Let us begin our second journey. It's in the other direction – into the future. Right? Right. Doors to Automatic. First stop – 2090, a hundred years from now. Even the most long-lived of us will have left the earth by then. Many years before that, the priest will have prayed for us: 'Eternal rest grant to them, O Lord.' And the people, the living people, will join in: 'And may perpetual light shine on them and may his soul, may her soul and the souls of all the faithful departed, rest in peace.' One hundred years from now, eternal rest, perpetual light, peace – with God's help, these will be ours. But what do they mean? Where will we be and what will we be doing one hundred years from now, or one thousand or ten thousand? We shall be with God and we will be doing what we do at the beginning of every eucharistic prayer - we will be saying, 'It is right to give him thanks and praise.'

You see, heaven is really a eucharistic prayer, an eternal thanksgiving - it's thanks, *go raibh míle maith agat, 's go raibh míle míle maith agat. Cead míle buíochas do Dhia.* Heaven is delight in God's goodness. We will delight in all the goodness there ever was and we will be reunited with those we love. Think of the rejoicing. Journey's end in lovers' meetings, and all the journeys will be over. Children and parents whom death divided will be together again. The husbands and wives who cried for each other will laugh as when first they loved. Friends long absent from each other's company will meet to part no more.

One of the loveliest and saddest tributes to a friend was the poem the Greek Callimachus wrote for his friend Heraclitus:

> They told me, Heraclitus, they told me you were dead,
> They brought me bitter news to hear and bitter tears to shed.
> I wept as I remembered how often you and I
> Had tired the sun with talking and sent him down the sky.

In heaven these two friends will talk forever, and the sun will never go down the sky.

And in heaven we'll see all the meanings of all the things that puzzled us on earth. We say here on earth, 'Why did God …?' and, 'Wouldn't ye think God would …?' and it's only faith that keeps us going and often that faith is put to the pin of its collar. In heaven, one hundred years from now, we'll have no faith at all because there will be no place for faith; we will see the answers to all our question in the light of the Beatific Vision.

There will be no Mass in heaven either, for the Mass will have done its work; it will have brought us home to God. The only part of the Mass that will remain will be the thanks and praise. So as we say, 'It is right to give him thanks and praise', we are practising for heaven, saints in training. For our final vocation is to be God's eucharistic people, people who see good and say '*Cead míle buíochas do Dhia.*'

That's heaven – but it's time we came back to earth. And you'll say in the meantime (and time can be very mean), 'What do I give thanks and praise for?' There's every kind of trouble in the world, the tortured man, the woman without a home, child hungry, child abused, child killed. It is hard to give him thanks and praise. The litany of woes is long: we have a lot of complaining to do, and God has a lot of explaining to do. It is right to give him thanks and praise? Yet Christ did. He gave God thanks and praise even as he stood on the edge of betrayal, of torture and of death. He shrank from what he must go through and he was in the dark for explanations and he would ask God, 'Why have you forsaken me?' And still at the edge of this precipice he gave thanks and praise to God.

Why? Not for the suffering and pain and death – oh no!

But for what he saw above and beyond it – the everlasting and limitless goodness of God. He knew all the bad there was and he could feel the drops of evil like a black rain on his hands and head but he knew that the black rain would be lost and drowned in the ocean of God's love. And so with the bread in his hand, at the edge of his agony and in the teeth of death, Christ gave thanks and praise.

The eucharistic mind is the mark of Christ. Christ had a thanksgiving mind and the eucharistic mind sees all the good there is and loves it, and sees all the bad there is and is sorry for it. And Christ pities the fallen and forgives the failure, and will absorb our evil into his own body, so that the world's sin will be washed away in his blood and bad Fridays will become good.

But the eucharistic mind does not come cheap – it did not come cheap to Christ, and Mary paid dear for her Magnificat. It does not come easy to us either. We will say, 'It is right to give him thanks and praise', and if we say it without thinking, it's easy, but when we mean it, we will sometimes struggle to say it and to see its meaning.

But even as we struggle, the eucharistic mind of God is giving thanks for us. Maybe you'd be surprised at that – that God would be saying thanks for you. But you know everything good we do only reflects the goodness of God. And even our thanks and praise – it was from God we learned it. God rejoices over goodness everywhere. It's his trademark. It's the first thing we learn about God in the Bible – 'God saw that it was good.' And when God sees your goodness he rejoices over you: 'This is my beloved son, my beloved daughter, in whom I am well pleased.' God gives thanks for all the goodness gathered here – the goodness that made you travel to Knock and the years it took you with all the giving, and struggling and minding and working and putting up with. Only God could thank you enough for what you have done and do. And one day God will begin his preface by saying to you, 'It is right to give you thanks and praise.' Thanks is a two-way street and we never travel on it but we meet God coming down the other way.

So tonight, let the trouble slip off your shoulders, let the wonder of God's love and mercy run into your mind, into your heart, into your soul. Let thanks, Eucharist, take over your face and your spirit – for you are God's and God is yours, and all shall be well and all manner of thing shall be well. God loves you and there's no more to be said. But what shall we do with this God of ours? Oh, it is right to give him thanks and praise. *Cead míle buíochas do Dhia.* Right? Right.

Death: The Endgame

Vol. 40, No. 6, June 1989

Tuesday is All Saints. Wednesday is All Souls. I always liked All Saints – it was family and fun and apples and nuts and bracks and the ring – life. I hated All Souls. The weight of death was on the day. It was the time when you could gain a plenary indulgence for a dead person each time you made a visit to the church and prayed for them. And you always thought of one more person and you'd feel guilty if you didn't pray for them. So back in you went for another visit. You carried the burden of the dead on All Souls. It was a bit like Ash Wednesday – a black day. I suppose the real reason, the deep reason, is that it reminds us of death, and we don't always like to think about that. But now and again we should think about it and some day we must all think of it. No one is let off the grave. So a couple of times a year the Church reminds us and about one hundred times a year the funeral bell in the church reminds us. The Church reminds us because it has something to say about death and if it didn't have something to say about it, it would have nothing to say about life. But what it has to say about death isn't frightening. On the contrary, it is comforting, reassuring and hopeful. If we had no religion, no faith, then death would be hopeless, but as an old prayer says, 'Blessed be God who has placed hope in the grave.'

So the Church is comforting and reassuring because it is sure of God's love for us and it wants us to be sure of God's love and so, not to be afraid – God's love for us should take away our fear. But the Church is wise and faces facts, and now and again it would like us to use death to make us reflect on life – to make us thoughtful. And during November when we pray for the dead, maybe we'd think of the fact that this life isn't infinite, isn't eternal for any of us. We know that, of course, but we don't always think of it. And what difference would that make? Well one of the Eastern religions says when you think about it, if you imagine you have died, it makes you more care-full – not careful, but care-full – aware of the love you have for your family and your friends, and it stops you letting little unimportant things come between you. It makes you more aware of the everyday miracles of love and care and beauty that bless us. When you think of the shortness of life, you live better, because time is limited, and you don't want to waste it on hate or bitterness.

And we don't always realise this. In a way life is like a game of snooker, you know, when you see Dennis Taylor, Steve Davis and Alex Higgins playing on TV these winter nights – the green table, the triangle of fifteen red balls and the colours, yellow and green and brown and blue and pink and black. So many of them on the table, you'd think the game would never end. Snooker is like life that way. You'd think it would never end. There are so many reds you can be careless with them and the colours keep popping back into play. No shortage. Then suddenly there are only three reds left, then two and all too soon the last red is gone and now there are only the colours. They had seemed to be everlasting and now they go one by one and they don't come back. It's like the fading of the light of a nice November evening. The yellow goes, like the sun, then the green like the grass, then the brown like the earth, and the blue goes like the blue of the sky, and the pink like the sunset and then only the black is left, the black of night, the black of death. The black goes. The game is over. Death has cleared the table. It's very like life and it looks as if death is the winner.

Ah, but not quite. When the black is gone, there is still one ball left – the white – white for the dawn that will come again; white for the Resurrection; white that is the Church's colour of victory; the white that will begin the new game, the white of hope that remains when the black is gone, the white that will gather all the reds again and all the colours for the new game.

You know white was put on you at baptism – a white robe, as a sign that you were a new creation, clothed in Christ; that's the prayer that was said over you – a white garment, it said, that would see you safely into heaven. That's Christ's promise – and he makes a further one that we shall be reunited in happiness around him in heaven. So may we be made worthy of the promises of Christ.

But, of course, people are afraid, afraid of what is after death. Some people are afraid there isn't a God, some people are afraid there is. We're often afraid I think because we can't imagine – we can't imagine heaven and we can't imagine God. We think we can see everything but in truth our sight is very limited. Someone said we are like a baby in the womb. If someone said to the unborn baby, 'You can't stay here you know. In a few weeks you will be born – you'll have to leave this place, you'll have to die out of here.' The baby might say, 'But I don't want to leave here; I'm warm, loved and happy here. I don't want to be what you call born, or what I call die out of this place.'

But the baby is born. And finds faces that love him, hands that care for him, children that play with him, welcome him, smile at him. He grows, enjoys, and loves. And then he learns that he must leave this place too. He must die, or, as the gospel says, be born into new life. Again he might say, 'But I don't want to – I'm happy here. I'm loved and I love this world, the warm fire on my face, sunrise and sunset, green fields, the colours of flowers, clean water and my own people. All this I love and don't want to leave. I don't want to die.'

But he dies. Is God, who created the love and beauty in the world he has left, suddenly going to become different? Oh no, God's nature does not change, and God's word is true. The baby, the man, will meet in his new life love and beauty, beyond all our imagining, and meet again all those he had loved, and lost in death.

That's what I believe. That's the way I see things now. So I see November differently now. I still rejoice in All Saints but I'm no longer afraid of All Souls – amn't I thinking of my own and happy for their happiness whether they be All Saints or All Souls? So November is really Easter – new life and heaven – achieved fully for All Saints, achieved certainly for All Souls, and promised for God's people on earth.

So today and on Tuesday and on Wednesday, let us pray in the Mass with thanks for All Saints and with love for All Souls and with sure hope for ourselves.

Penance: Point of No Return

Vol. 40, No. 6, June 1989

It may seem like an odd thing to say but we are here to welcome Christ, to welcome him back. The gospel I read you (Luke 3:2–6) told of the old preparation in rough country for the coming of a king, the making of a road so that the king could come and welcome. The straightening of the crooked, the smoothing of the rough, the levelling of the high and low. The king we wait for is coming to us this evening and we are rough country. The heart's a wilderness, with valleys of darkness and black hills, and we meet tonight to pray together with and for one another that Christ the King may come and bring light to the black and the dark and the wilderness in each of us and in all of us.

In one of our nicer phrases of welcome, we say about somebody, 'You're a cure for sore eyes!' Tonight we are gathered here to welcome Christ and to say to him 'We're glad to see you – you're a cure for sore eyes!'

That's why Christ came, anyway – to cure sore eyes, eyes whose vision had faded or maybe gone out altogether, to cure hearts that were sore with loving the wrong things, to heal hurt minds and bring light to souls gone dark.

So we gather to welcome him because we need him; we need someone to make us new again, to give us a new start, new heart. The clay is gone dry on our hands. We're like grubby ten-pence pieces, dirtied by too many hands, darkened and sticky from too many purses and pockets – we need to be showered again by mercy and love. Take away the staleness, Lord, take it all away and change us and set us free and make us fresh again.

And because he knew us and the way we'd be and feel he said: Come to me all of you who labour and are heavily burdened, come to me when you're struggling and weighed down and I will refresh you. And because he loved us he came to us. And because he loved us he looked for us. And because he loved us he died for us. So we gather, we go over like the shepherds to Bethlehem to welcome Christ the cure for sore eyes, Christ the cure for sore lives.

There is no need to be afraid. He's not that sort of king. Bethlehem was meant to take away fear. For what's in Bethlehem but what's calm and domestic – even the animals are that – and happy. There is no threat in a child and a young mother and a carpenter who can't take his eyes off them. And you don't even have to knock, for there's no door.

So here we are, Lord, a strange welcoming committee. You know who we are. Some of us with good consciences and some of us with bad, some of us content, some discontent, the certain and the uncertain, Christians called by your name and little like you, Christians by conviction and Christians by convention, some who believe and some of us who half believe and maybe some who think they disbelieve. We have promised much often and delivered little, we have broken promises and broken words and broken friendships.

You know where we have come from – from great loneliness or from lives of quiet comfort or from confusion and distress, from homes that are happy or homes in pain, from relationships in great disorder, some of us at peace, some of us needing your help even to name the sin that shames us.

Here we are, Lord, each with a different story, a different history. We stand before you alike in this, that we are all in the wrong with you or with one another. We all need your grace and your forgiveness. You are our hope and our saviour.

You stretched out your hands once, Lord, to men who were sinking. We reach out to you now in the same need and the same hope. You stretched out your hands, Lord, once on a cross, for men condemned. Lord, here we are again, the guilty; forgive us again, Lord of the nailed hands. Lord, you once held out your hands on an Easter Sunday and said, 'My peace be with you.' Lord, give us your peace. Lord, we have gone astray like sheep: our eyes stray, our minds stray, our feet stray, our hearts stray. Lord, have pity on the lost. Find us, mind us, bring us back to you.

We are about to receive the gift of Christ and we are about to give the gift of our selves. We mightn't think that any great bargain but it's the only thing God wants from us, that we might come to him just as we really are – not the me I show the world or the marvellous me I dream about but the real me, the realest, the truest me I can give – to come before God, kind and loving and merciful and say, 'This is me, Lord. I love you, please forgive me and help me.' And in that love, his love and ours, all that is bad in us is changed for joy and peace.

He gives us back to ourselves no longer scattered and broken and divided individuals, sin-scarred, but instead now reunited with him, open and sure and strong. We begin again to see the meaning of our lives, and the meaning of those we love and the meaning of those we have offended and hurt and betrayed. And with new vision comes not only new meaning but a new strength – the strength of God's grace once again alive in us. And we who were lost are found, and we who were dead come to life again, and we rejoice in God and God rejoices in us.

That's the end of the story of the Prodigal Son. That story that began with a departure and ended with return and welcome and joy. I want to finish by telling you an old Jewish story said to be older than the Prodigal Son. In a way it prefigures what we are doing at this moment. It's a story of return – the word the Jews used for repentance, the turning back to the God you had left and perhaps forgotten or were just at odds with.

The king's son left the palace in guilt because of wrong he had done and went into exile – far from home, away from the love he could not face. But his father couldn't forget him and he sent messengers to ask him to come back. The boy answered that the way was long and dangerous and he'd be afraid. And the father sent word that he would go halfway to meet him, but the boy still refused, saying: 'The woods are dark, we might miss each other in the dark woods and then I should be lost forever.' But his father said: 'Sing as you come and I will sing as I go and we will hear each other's song and meet and come back together singing.'

May we, this night, walk back with God and turn for home in his company and his peace.

'I don't go any more ...'

Vol. 40, No. 6, June 1989

How do you feel when you hear someone isn't going to Mass any more, or when they tell you themselves: 'Ah well, I don't bother any more, I gave that up when I went to England, when I left home'? Maybe a friend of yours, maybe somebody in the family. 'Ah well, I don't bother any more.' How do you feel when you hear it? The reasons can be different. They can even be different from what they tell you: 'I don't believe any more', which might mean 'I don't believe any more', or could mean 'I can't get up on Sunday morning' or 'The other fellows don't go' or 'There's this fellow I'm seeing and he's married' – or indeed it may be and very honestly, 'It doesn't mean much to me.'

But how do you feel when you hear it? A bit saddened? A bit afraid? Do you find it's a small blow to your faith? Do you feel a bit of a shake in your own spiritual foundations, a brick go loose in the wall of your own belief? Is it – especially if you are young – harder to get up the next Sunday, easier to turn into a lounge and feel less guilty? And if you're an older person, especially a father or mother, do you worry for the faith of your own – or maybe remember when one of them said it to you and pray again that God will bring them back? How do you feel when you hear it? A bit more alone maybe, some bit of a chill wind touching you, and you button up the coat of your belief, turn up the collar of your faith and keep out what you are afraid of. And he's such a nice lad, she's such a nice girl – at school with me, nice then and still nice.

When a friend stops going, somehow their leaving makes you feel lonely, separated, unprotected. 'Will you also go away?' Even Christ looks like that in this gospel (Twenty-first Sunday of the Year, Cycle B), lonely, separated, unprotected, pathetic. The crowds he had fed, who had followed him, can't accept what he tells them about the Eucharist – that it's the bread from heaven, that he who eats it will never die, that the Eucharist is himself. They could accept that he'd raise someone from the dead – didn't they see him? They could accept that he'd multiply five loaves into bread for thousands – didn't they eat it? But this, this bread from heaven, eternal life, the body and blood of Christ – this is too much, who could believe this? We have only his word for it.

So, many of his disciples left him, stopped going with him. He stood there and they went from him, by him, one or two first and then in crowds, one borrowing the courage to leave from another – because we depend on one another for our unbelief as for our belief – streaming past him they went, until there was only a handful left. And Christ turned to the twelve and said, half-ironically, half-pathetically, 'Will you also go away?'

It's a lonely moment – the moment when friends desert you. Anyone who has ever watched or been a little boy, when friends refuse to let him into their game, will know the feeling. Anyone who has ever watched a little girl cut out by her companions, left out of the secrets and out of the play will know the feeling – 'we don't want you'. If you have ever seen or been left out like that you'll know Christ's feeling at that moment. 'Will you also go away?'

I suppose it's a question that is in a way put to us, put up to us every time we hear of someone who has gone away. Christ puts the question to us then: 'Will you also go away?' and we have to gather our faith and square the shoulders of our belief to stay with Christ. And we know that the question will come again, because there will always be someone else who says, 'This is intolerable, how could anyone accept it?'

But it does give a new meaning to your Communion, if you think of Christ saying to us just at the moment before Communion, 'Will you also go away?' And you don't go, you stay. You hear the words 'Body of Christ', you say 'Amen', you receive Christ. He gives you the gift of himself. But you have given him the gift of your faith. And even more it gives new meaning to your Mass.

Your presence at Mass, even when you are tired or uninterested or feel bored, maybe even more when you are like that – your presence at Mass has vast meaning. It is a statement made by you, that you believe in Christ's word, that this is the bread of life, that Christ is God come down from heaven, that this is Christ, Body and Blood. It's a statement made not just in speech, but in body, not just the faith of your mouth, but the faith of your feet. For you're here, you have not gone áway. He has put the question, 'Will you also go away?' and here you are, the very answer he was looking for. Your presence at Mass is never less than that. It is a compliment to Christ, as Peter's answer was that day, and Christ never forgets a compliment.

But what of those who went away? Well, you know, they were able to believe their eyes when they saw the other miracles. What they couldn't believe was his word. And Christ didn't try to stop them. He didn't take back a word, never said, 'Oh, I didn't quite mean that' – because he did mean it and they knew he did, and they knew that if they were to be fully members of his Eucharist group, his Church, they must accept his word on this challenge to believe.

And they couldn't and they left and he never shouted 'stop'! And he never blamed them, because he still loved them and always would and would still care for them and would die for them and he did. And what of those who go away now? Our own, family, friends – Christ doesn't blame them either and he still loves them, they're still his as they are still ours, and he died for them, and he knows all the good that's in them and rejoices in the good they do. And we must too, and not blame, for no one knows the force of another's temptations, the doubts, the difficulties, the perplexities of situations.

They are still Christ's concern and his care – he can't forget them – for they are part of his family, even when they no longer walk with him. And if they are his then they must be ours. They must come to Mass in us, they must be part of our prayers, they must share in our Communions. If people are starving in the Sudan, we know that those who have should help. If people are starved of the bread of life, those who have must help too. So our Communion is never just ours. All those who can't or won't walk with Christ, must be carried in our prayers and in our love. You see, the weight of the others comes on those who remain. Christ makes demands on his friends and on their friendship. Faith is a privilege and it brings obligations.

So, at the end, there was Peter – the common man – answering for himself and for the others and for me and for you and for everyone at Mass here now, or anywhere this day, 'Will you also go away?' and Peter answered, 'Lord, who would we go to? You have the message of eternal life and we believe.'

In a minute we'll stand and say the Creed. And there are a lot of things in the Creed, but it will say no more than Peter said when Christ asked him to stand up and be counted. We could use it as a prayer. 'Lord, who would we go to? You have the message of eternal life and we believe.'

The crowds are gone;

Christ and Peter standing there – a question, 'Will you also go away?'

Christ and Peter standing there – an answer, 'Lord, who would we go to? You have the message of eternal life and we believe.'

With that picture in our minds and those words in our ears, let us stand and answer for ourselves.

Homilies for December

Vol. 42, No. 11, November 1991

First Sunday of Advent

Thurber once had a cartoon of one man saying to another: 'Christmas has us by the throat again.' For the preacher, often happy on Christmas morning to say 'just a few words and not spoil your Christmas', it is rather Advent which has us by the throat, the preaching place, where else? And will we talk again about the commercialisation of Christmas, and preparation, and the good news, and too much drink. Probably and expectedly and rightly – but not with a whimper but a bang if we follow today's gospel. For the Church begins the year with all barrels blazing, the storms of *Great Expectations* and *Wuthering Heights*, *King Lear* and *The Cruel Sea* all together, and yet above the elements Christ appears and above the clamour and the roaring his voice assures us – stand erect, hold your head high, stand with confidence.

It's a cosmic gospel. 'Cosmic' is an adjective we usually associate with 'proportions' or 'disaster'. It's a word which dwarfs the human being, a word which sees us very tiny, very weak and running frightened or lying dead in a disaster of cosmic proportions. But this cosmic gospel puts 'cosmic' in its place, because it introduces someone greater than the cosmic – the very Lord of Time and Space. And his followers participate in his power and so they can stand with confidence. This is the Son of Man, and his brothers and sisters will find that through him disaster is liberation.

This gospel is really like a film which shows the end and then begins the story. Over the next few weeks we make our way to the child. But this gospel, this last-first chapter, tells us who this baby will be – Lord , Saviour, Almighty God, Son of Man, and one of us. The mystery of the Incarnation begins.

But we're on our way to meet the child. We're most like the Three Wise Men at this time. Perhaps they're setting out, or on their way, leaving home or in the desert, but they're six weeks away from meeting the child. We're four weeks away. The wise men are preparing or prepared – thinking about presents.

('What would you think about a bit of gold as a present, Casper?' 'Well, I am bringing a bit of gold myself, Melchior.' 'Oh, all right, maybe he'd like some myrrh.' 'Good idea, always useful – his mother will like it anyway.')

They're thinking maybe about food and drink, have they enough, where will they get it? They're thinking about the dangers in the weeks ahead and how they'll cope with the journey and mind their camels, and how they'll get on with each other, and who they will meet at the end of it all, and will it make much difference to them. Will they be glad or sorry when Christmas comes? All questions we can ask and will ask and do ask – except about the camels, and of course the wise men didn't know the meeting would be called Christmas. So they are very like us, preparing and on the way. And they followed a star. One small light in the cosmos.

We have our own little light – small in the sanctuary, the first candle lit on the Advent wreath. This one candle is a cosmic sign, a star set lighting on the dark circle of the wreath – not just a good deed in a naughty world, but good news in an unredeemed world, the Lord of Space and Time is on his way and we are on ours. This meeting is set for Bethlehem in Judah, for Claremorris in Mayo, for Dublin, London, New York, Delhi, Sydney, Tokyo, in four weeks time. And meeting is a God.

The circle is an age-old symbol for eternity – like the marriage ring. A ring has no end. So the circle is a sign of eternity and of God who is eternal, the God of the ages, the Lord of the rings. From God, the circle, comes Christ, the white central candle, but he won't be here till Christmas, so it's not lit till then. But he's here as promised.

The evergreens stand for eternal life. Evergreens don't die in winter and green is the colour of hope. So they stand there, strong immortal signs set against all winters, seasonal, nuclear and the winter of our discontent. They stand as God's promise to us through Christ that we'll be evergreen. We will not die. 'The one who believes in me will never die,' said Christ. So the green of their hope is the picture, the colour to match the confidence of the gospel today – hold your head high.

And as the gospel is at once cosmic and personal, so the wreath.

For the purple candles domesticate eternity. There's work to be done on earth, in this house, in this heart. Purple is the Church's colour of renewal. It's the colour of the Church's apron. The Church always puts on the purple apron when it's getting the house ready, when it's getting the cobwebs out of corners and polishing the spoons – getting ready for someone coming. It does it at Lent for Easter, for the returning Christ. It does it at Advent for Christmas and the coming Christ. So we have to get ready, for he's coming. There's cleaning to be done. We can't leave the house like this.

I like the Advent wreath. It tells an extraordinary story, the history of the world in a way, and not cosmic disaster, but cosmic celebration. But what I like about it is the light – first one candle, then another and another and another, and then them all. It's like as if Christ was in a car a long way off and you're looking out for him and you look into the dark night, and far away you see a light. Is it a car? Is it him? By the second Sunday – two lights – it's definitely a car and by the third Sunday it's coming this way. On the fourth Sunday it's pulling into the house and then – oh it's him all right. Christ steps out. The white candle is lit and it's Christmas. Like a car, or a star. But that's four weeks away. Hand me the apron.

Second Sunday of Advent

Oyez! Oyez! Another noisy gospel. Two of the great God-voices calling to God's people. The Baptist proclaiming. Isaiah crying out. They're calling for attention, they want to be heard and heeded. They're men with a message and they're on fire with it. Repentance for the forgiveness of sins. Prepare a way for the Lord.

They think it's good news. It sounds grim to us – penance, straightening crooked ways and smoothing rough ones. Isn't Christmas for celebrating? Why is the Church such a killjoy, a spoilsport? It does it at Easter with Lent, and here it is, at it again with Advent. Ah, let's celebrate with an easy conscience. After all it's office party time, mistletoe time and a bird never flew on one wing. We'll be dead long enough.

Hold! – but if it's drink you are talking about, maybe 'we'll be dead soon enough' might be a better motto if you are going to drink and drive or cycle or walk on Advent or Christmas roads. One for the road? or, as Louis MacNeice wrote,

One for the grave? Hold! The Church isn't for death but for life and it isn't sport it wants to spoil or joy it wants to kill. How could it be against the excitement of Christmas when it is spending four weeks building up that excitement?

Excitement comes easy at Christmas, thank God. There's the excitement of getting ready, getting the house clean, getting food – cakes, pudding, mince pies – excitement of getting gifts, giving and receiving socks and soap, excitement of people coming home, Pat and Mick and Mary Kate. And it is all a reflection of how the excitement started, the first excitement at the first Christmas. The coming of Christ who was to be Lord, the bread of life, and drink, wine or water. The coming of Christ who was a gift from God to us. The coming of Christ who was to bring people together and make the homeless at home – a huge communion of friends. So the socks and the cakes and the plane into Knock and the train into Claremorris are real signs of Christmas and that's easy to see. They can be real signs of Christ too, but that's easy to forget.

So the Church is trying to make us remember, stop us being thoughtless and make us thoughtful. It tries every way it can – with colour, did you notice the purple vestments? With light, did you notice the second candle? With words, did you hear the prophet foretelling the coming of Christ, and did you hear John the Baptist who introduced Christ?

Maybe Christ has a harder time getting here these days. Maybe the mountains of advertising, the hills of sound are higher than ever and need more laying low. Maybe the winding ways of super-markets are very slow to straighten. They can wrap us around until we're so wrapped up in ourselves that we're like a Christmas presentation ourselves – all lovely paper and strings outside and the same old biscuits inside. The world's Advent to the world's Christmas can insulate us against Christ who is calling to us in the needs of others, the hungry, the beaten, the down, our own, next door. We can be like a good piece of electrical cable, well insulated. You pick it up, you feel nothing. The Church this day is trying to pull off the insulation. Without the insulation we might get a shock, we might feel the electricity of Christ's coming, his shocking need that takes flesh in an Irish kitchen that has no heat, or an Ethiopian face that has no food. And when we think of that, we might, as we say, be very put out. But then the only way to let Christ in is to put yourself out.

So the Church tears at our insulation, stripping us to the bare wires. Killjoy – not for the people who will be warmed by the kindness of our restraint, a very live joy for the people who get fed by the generosity of our temperance.

The magazine *Newsweek* this year summed up a certain kind of modern religion. 'Heaven, by this creed, is never having to say "no" to yourself and God is never having to say you're sorry.' This is not the heaven in which the angels will sing and this is not the God who comes at Christmas. The child who comes, like every child, will ask questions and you might be afraid that some of them would be awkward ones. But the first question he asks is the most important one and the one that lights up the answers to all the others – 'What would you like yourself for Christmas?' Giorgio? The leather jacket? An even higher-fi? A feed of drink? Or would it be even nicer to have a happy Christmas, a happy home, peace there, kindness, no drunkenness, no fighting, laughter, joy, consideration?

He's very real, this child, not a dreamer, not dreaming of a white Christmas. He comes to give a Christmas worthy of his name. He knows as well as any one of us that the greatest trouble in families this Christmas will be over money and drink. Money – not everyone will have enough, and what might be enough can be squeezed dry in a family where some make unreasonable demands. Money – generosity, especially the generosity of restraint, will create happiness where selfishness will bring misery and rows. And drink – too much spent on drink or too much drink will spoil Christmas for whole housefuls. As the man said, 'America in the pub, Ethiopia at home', and Christmas will mean worry or want or war in the house. The generosity of temperance not only saves lives, it also gives life – Christlike.

So you want good news? So how to get ready for a Happy Christmas? The voices are trying to tell us. Listen. Oyez, Oyez, 'Prepare the way of the Lord.' Not the other way.

Third Sunday of Advent

Someone's coming. 'A feeling of expectancy', says the gospel. 'People on tiptoe with expectation', somebody else translates it. Someone's coming. Does he live up to expectation?

People see Christmas differently. This Christ, whatever else he did, fulfilled one prophecy 'that out of many hearts thoughts would be revealed. Dickens has Scrooge's nephew say,

> I have always thought of Christmas time when it has come round as a good time – a kind, forgiving, charitable, pleasant time; the only time I know in the long calendar of the year when men and women seem by one consent to open their shut-up hearts freely and to think of people below them as if they really were fellow passengers to the grave and not another race of creatures bound on other journeys.

A Christmas Carol, Charles Dickens

On the other hand a man: 'I'm seventy-one and I dread Christmas and every year makes it worse.' And two women I overheard on a bus in Dublin talking about Christmas. One wished it was over. 'It's only for children,' she said, 'and with the price of toys I'm glad all mine are grown up.' The other woman said, 'It's such a sad time and everything bad that ever happened in our family happened at Christmas – me father died, me brother John had the accident in Australia, me sister's child got burnt. I wish it was over.'

Not everybody's on tiptoe, and what can I say? I can't take away the pain of life, 'of the long agony which is old age'. I can't take away the memories of happier days which are bittersweet now because they remind us of the joy that was and never will be more. I can't take them away and He won't. They are part of the human condition. Has Christ anything to say to that?

I remember once congratulating a man on a very happy occasion. He really was very happy and then he said 'but if only she were here herself'. He meant his wife who had died some years before. Then he said, 'That's the trouble with life. There's always a bloody "but".'

> The fairest things have fleetest end,
> Their scent survives their close.
> But the Rose's scent is bitterness
> To him who loved the Rose ...

There's that 'but' again. What had this Christ we wait for on tiptoe, to say?

The holly has red berries and it has thorns. Christ came to pull the thorns from the holly. He took them, he wore them so that we'd know he knew the feel of them, and the feel of us when they make us bleed. He came with a promise, that he would finally take away the bloody 'but'. But first he lived through it. That's the good news that finishes today's gospel. The news of the Incarnation – call it Christmas. The news that the all-powerful God has come as one of us, that he knows our pain, understands our pain, and promises that our goodbyes will not be forever.

God really became one of us. We know what it's like to be us, but until Christ we didn't know what it's like to be God, not really. Before Christ we had only words. Christ drew the picture, in fact he put flesh on it. It's one thing to say 'God cares.' It's another when God says, 'What'll we do with these people? I'm very worried about them, they're famished with the hunger – have ye any food there we could give them?' It's one thing to say God forgives sin. It's another to say, 'Imagine the father longing for the lad who left home and made a fool of himself. Imagine the father longing for him to come home and running to meet him and dressing him up and having a huge party for him and any time the lad tries to explain, the father says "Not a word now. It's all over."' And it's one thing to say that God is merciful but it's another thing when men are going to kill a woman because they caught her with a man, and God says, 'Take it easy now. Did ye ever do anything wrong yourselves?' And they get ashamed and they leave her, and God says to her, 'It's all right now. Don't do any more wrong.' And it's one thing to say 'God loves you' and another thing entirely when God comes to live like you and die for you to prove his love.

So that's the good news. That's the Incarnation. God becoming one of us so that God can say to us, 'I know how you feel' – because he does, because Jesus felt like that himself, down, up, middling, afraid, beat out. It's God becoming one of us so that we can say to God, 'Do you know the way I feel? – I'm down, I'm out, I'm crucified with this pain', and he understands because he was like us, like that too.

And if you're seventy-one and dreading Christmas – or any other age, when Christmas brings the expectation of pain and not the expectation of joy, when you're not on tiptoe but flat-footed, what can I say except to say that beyond the tinsel there's the truth that Christ came to rescue us from the dread and to give meaning to the pain? Maybe we have to let go of the trappings, the false-faced happiness, the professionally cheerful programmes, the gaily wrapped presumption that everybody should be happy because there is so much to eat and so much to drink. Maybe we have to let go of the trappings and go on our knees in the stable and say, 'I believe your promise. I'm yours, you're mine, and please help me now.' That's all I can say – but it's the truth, so help me God.

Fourth Sunday of Advent

We're at the sign of the four candles. The focus of the liturgy softens. This bit takes place in the kitchen. This isn't John the Baptist proclaiming to soldiers and tax gatherers. The voices this morning are softer. Women's voices delighted, giving each other their news, good news. If there's a Women's Christmas on 6 January to celebrate birth, maybe this is Woman's Advent to celebrate pregnancy.

But what was told in the kitchen will soon be news for the city and for the world, like the Pope's blessing. The delight, the congratulations, have been played a million times between women in this world's history. That much is the same and every child is unique, but this child is God and this woman is the Mother of God.

What would you say? Would you be lost for words? Could you put it in a sentence? Elizabeth, countrywoman from the hills, could and did. 'Of all women you are the most blessed and blessed is the fruit of your womb.' The momentous bringing forth the memorable. Grace under pressure but inspired too, for wasn't she filled with the Holy Spirit? So she gave us the words we use, the words that millions have used, in the Hail Mary. 'Hail, full of grace, the Lord is with you,' the angel Gabriel had said briefly and superbly. He might have said, 'Follow that.' And Elizabeth did with equal inspiration. We give thanks for a woman with words marvellous enough to greet the Word and to celebrate Mary.

And Mary waits while Elizabeth speaks. She was good at waiting, even in difficult times. It was something she knew now and would again. I think of her in that first Advent and it must have been a hard enough time for her. Oh, she had put herself in God's hands, and willingly. 'Behold the handmaid of the Lord,' she had said. 'Be it done unto me according to his word.' But that didn't mean the absence of anxiety or the stopping up of humanity in Mary. Humanity worries and Mary had plenty to worry about. She had great news and news not easily shared. Did God send her to Elizabeth because he knew her woman's need for a best friend?

Mary didn't know there would be angels singing. She had no vision of what Christmas would be. She couldn't but wonder about it, and this morning's gospel happened because she wanted someone to talk to.

It brings us close to her. So often we follow in her footsteps and go across our own hill country to meet her because we want someone to talk to. We all lay claim to Mary. Somehow we can feel out of touch, perhaps even happily out of touch with God. We can feel God like a judgement at moments but we feel Mary won't judge us. She's our gate of heaven, a way through when every other door is closed against us or locked by us. She is calm and good and wise. She knows. You could talk to her and she'd clear your mind for you. She's, as we say and it's hard to better an angel, full of grace.

A Gaelic poet called her 'Mary of the God-Mind' ('Hey the Gift, Ho the Gift', unknown poet). A French poet imagines God the Father talking of her and saying, 'I'm sometimes for justice, she's always for mercy.' They are all just different ways of expressing our delight in her, and we're not too wrong in that for the Church sees God delighting in her too. And she is full of grace. And she is the Mother of God. And she is one of us.

Christmas Day
A day of wonder. Still a day of wonder, and full of mystery. There's the mystery of the ordinary, and the mystery of the eternal. God is domesticated and the world's history begins again in a cave. It is mystery and mixture. Evelyn Underhill wrote to someone once, 'I do hope your Christmas has had a little touch of Eternity in among the rush and pitter-patter and all. It always seems such a mixing of this world and the next – but that after all is the idea.'

I met a young man I once taught. He was a couple of years married and I hadn't met him since he had got married. He was telling me about himself and the girl he married, who she was, and about the house they had built on a bit of land his father gave him – the usual things. Then his face broke into a grin and he winked at me and he said, 'An' I have a small daughtereen too.' That's usual enough too, but it's very special to the one who feels it. I think Mary knew how he felt as he said it. She felt the same way once herself, and tonight I think she asks us in again to share her joy in her small son.

The old painters who show Mary kneeling, head bent over her little son catch at the same time the two mysteries, the ordinary, the girl in wonder and love as she looks at the child who is for her, and only for her, 'my baby'; and the eternal, the girl who looks quite literally in adoration at her baby and sees her God. It was a look that appeared only once ever on a human face, said a French philosopher, who said he was an atheist.

> That's what they celebrate everywhere,
> For its coming push tables together.

It's no day for separate tables. Jesus in himself joins God and the human race. The tables separated for so long have been pushed together by God and a woman. Christmas is a mixing of this world and the next, and each world mirrors the other. All the homecoming, the delight of people separated by oceans who meet in this small church tonight, the welcome home in families for members scattered worldwide, this joyful death to division is like a sign of what happened in that cave with no door. For the first Christmas was the beginning of restoration and reconciliation. The gate clanged shut in Eden, but here there is no door, and no shut-out people. Into this stable will come and welcome, shepherds and kings, unlearned and learned, animals and people. Here there is no forbidden fruit to divide God and his people, but the fruit of the woman's womb to delight God and his people. Mary's 'Yes' has not just contradicted but negatived Eve's 'No'. Here no man blames woman, and the animals are friends. This Son has come to give life and round this child there is peace.

Nobody's locked out or locked in here in Bethlehem. There's no hate and no fear and no threat. There's no loneliness for there's company and shared joy. There's no greed and no busyness. God sent his Son to help us stop running, to have us turn towards one another and have time for one another. We're not good listeners even to God, perhaps especially to God. We don't heed his Word. So the Word became flesh and dwelt amongst us. So that beside a baby we might stop and kneel, and maybe we might learn more on our knees than on our feet. He sent his Son to teach us, to reach us, because we are such slow learners. We might learn a lesson for this one day anyway, and not hurt anyone at home this day anyway, and be nice in the house to everyone this day anyway, and not spoil anyone's Christmas. If that happens our Christmas will have had at least a little touch of Eternity and Christ will have come to more than the crib. So 'let's go to Bethlehem and find our kneeling places.'

Feast of the Holy Family

It was a bad corner for Mary and Joseph. They say that after a journey you don't remember the good road, only the bad corners. Mary, like many another mother, still remembered years later the panic and the puzzlement. Most of the elements of the story are universal and perennial – a little boy lost, the assumption that they know where he is, misunderstandings, the search, the joy of finding. The twelve-year-old who is precocious and knows all the answers is universal and perennial too. The accusation from the Mother of God to the Son of God will raise an echo in the hearts of many parents and a knowing smile: 'What made you do a thing like that? Didn't you know …?'

The Incarnation was real all right. Someone said that for children their parents are slightly-out-of-date textbooks. Faced with Jesus' defence of himself – and defend himself is what he does in the best traditions of twelve-year-olds – Mary and Joseph seem to have had that sense of themselves – a little out-of-date and not quite up to this young man.

This gospel is remarkable for its story and for its sequel. The story is told vividly by someone who lived it and remembered it as if it was only yesterday. The sequel is vivid too – a vivid silence: 'I'll never forget these things', said Mary, 'and after that he grew up a lovely lad.' That sums up eighteen years of complete silence, what we call the hidden life.

Both the story and the silence are God's tribute to the work of parents, of families, of homes. The panic and the puzzle of Mary and Joseph are a kind of divine sympathy with the worry and frustration so many parents go through with these rebellious fragments of their own flesh which children are, from time to time, and from time immemorial. All parents say, 'God knows what we'll do with him/her.' At least this gospel tells us God knows the feeling. God knows it from Mary and from Joseph.

The last sentence of the gospel is God's reassurance to troubled parents. It's the reassurance of the ages but the God is the God of the ages. Today's parents are the children their parents worried about, and their parents are the children their parents worried about, and their parents are the children their grandparents worried about. An Assyrian tablet from 3800 BC says: 'The earth is degenerating in these latter days. There are signs that the world is speedily coming to an end. Bribery and corruption abound. The children no longer obey their parents.' The last sentence of today's gospel says, 'Jesus increased in wisdom, in stature and in favour with God and people.' It happens to a lot of young people who get lost at some point in their growing up.

And this is the Holy Family. What did God say by putting his Son in a family for thirty years? God could think of no better thing to do with him, could think of no better place for Jesus to be. I think the long silence of the years when Christ grew up is a strong statement by God of the holiness of the family where children are taught and minded and helped to grow in mind – 'wisdom'; in body – 'stature'; spiritually – 'in favour with God'; and emotionally – 'in favour with people'. The new curriculum is a very old curriculum designed by God, and he has chosen parents to teach it.

The holiness of the Holy Family is in one way special because of the meaning of Christ, his mission and identity, the meaning of Mary and Joseph in their relation to Christ and his mission. But the holiness which today's feast celebrates is the holiness of good people who care for each other, and work for each other, and sacrifice for each other. The holiness of Mary and Joseph doesn't come from the fact that they went carefully to the Temple to make their offering or that they went on pilgrimage to the Temple, though that care and prayer are part of holiness. The holiness of the Holy Family in this feast is the holiness evidenced in the love with which Mary tells her story, in the worry of love in Mary and Joseph. There is holiness in 'Your father and I' – I think Eve would have blamed Adam and Adam Eve. Mary and Joseph are together in love and worry, and there is holiness in their effort to understand, even when understanding was very difficult or beyond them. There is holiness in the consideration which Joseph showed Mary before Jesus was born, and his care for her afterwards – he perhaps personified for God and us the truth that the best thing a father can do for his children is be nice to their mother. There is holiness in the trust and friendship that knew Christ would be safe if he was with 'their relatives and acquaintances'. The whole gospel is alive with the holiness of relationship, the holiness of ordinary, sometimes frustrated, sometimes mistaken or misunderstood, but everlasting human love. I use the word 'everlasting' advisedly because in that love the human transcends it and touches the infinite love of God. Then the family is holy indeed and in all truth.

Finally, I think this is a gospel with God's smile upon it, his sympathy with loving memories, the treasures collected by the human heart for its furnishing. There's a simple poem which might have come out of the quiet years in Nazareth and Mary's memory of them, pondered upon and treasured:

Did Joseph carve some foolish thing
From extra bits of wood,
An ox, a camel, or a bird,
Because the Christ was good?

Oh, sometimes years are very long,
And sometimes years run fast,
And when the Christ had put away
Small, earthly things at last

And died upon a wooden cross
One afternoon in spring,
Did Mary find the little toy,
And sit … remembering?

'The Birthday',
Helen Welshimer